a gourmet cookbook for
diabetics

breakfast & brunch • appetizers & snacks
soups & salads • main dishes • side dishes • desserts

mc
rae
PUBLISHING

This book was conceived,
edited and designed by
McRae Publishing Ltd
London

www.mcraepublishing.co.uk

NOTE TO OUR READERS
Eating eggs or egg whites that are not completely cooked poses the
possibility of salmonella food poisoning. The risk is greater for
pregnant women, the elderly, the very young, and persons with
impaired immune systems. If you are concerned about salmonella,
you can use reconstituted powdered egg whites or pasteurized eggs.

Culinary Notebooks series

Project Director Anne McRae
Art Director Marco Nardi

A GOURMET COOKBOOK FOR DIABETICS
Photography: Shutterstock page 8 ©Alena Haurylik,
page 9 ©Yulia Davidovich, 11 tl ©Letterberry, tr ©Alena
Haurylik, bl ©mchin, br ©sarsmis; all other
photography by Brent Parker Jones
Text Nicola Greene
Editing Christine Price, Daphne Trotter
Food Styling Lee Blaylock
Food Preparation and Assistant
Stylists Mark Hockenhull, Milli Lee
Layouts Aurora Granata

ISBN 978-1-910122-35-8

Printed in China

contents

getting started

Here you will find more than 100 ideas for healthy and delicious dishes for diabetics and those who are at risk of developing type-2 diabetes in the future. Almost all the recipes are simple to prepare. To help you choose the right one, we have rated them for difficulty: 1 (simple), 2 (fairly simple), and 3 (challenging). In these two pages we have highlighted 25 of the most enticing dishes, just to get you started!

 QUICK

GREEN SMOOTHIES with sprouted wheat berries

FRESH PEA
hummus

PORTOBELLO burgers

GRILLED CAULIFLOWER
with pine nuts

FRESH FRUIT
cups

BERRY chia seed
pudding

SPICY TOFU
& VEGETABLE stir-fry

GRILLED EGGPLANT
with exotic spices

CHOCOLATE ZUCCHINI
muffins

 VEGETARIAN

GAZPACHO

SPECIAL OCCASIONS

SCALLOP skewers

VIETNAMESE shrimp rolls

CHILLED CUCUMBER SOUP with garlic shrimp

TURKEY BREAST IN PANCETTA with veggies

ANGEL FOOD CAKE with lavender & rose petals

MEXICAN EGGS & BEANS with avocado

SALADE niçoise

EDITOR'S CHOICE

TUNA BURGERS with roasties & salad

QUINOA biryani

CRÈME caramel

BEST BREAKFAST	BEST APPETIZER	BEST SOUP	BEST MAIN	BEST DESSERT

MUESLI & YOGURT parfait

CHICKEN STICKS with sweet chili sauce

MEATBALL soup

ROMAN-STYLE veal escalopes with broccoli

CHERRY & BLUEBERRY POTS with nut brittle

breakfast & brunch

CINNAMON OATMEAL with fresh fruit

1¼ cups (120 g) rolled oats
½ teaspoon ground cinnamon + extra, to dust
4 teaspoons brown sugar
2 cups (500 ml) skimmed milk
2 bananas, sliced
2 cups (300 g) fresh blueberries
1 (5-ounce/150-g) pot plain fat-free or low-fat yogurt

Serves 4 • Preparation 10 minutes • Cooking 4–5 minutes • Difficulty 1

1. Mix the oats, cinnamon, brown sugar, milk, and one banana in a medium saucepan over medium-high heat. Bring to a boil, stirring often. Decrease the heat to low and simmer for 4–5 minutes, stirring all the time.

2. Spoon the oatmeal into four serving bowls. Top with the remaining banana, the blueberries, a dollop of yogurt, and a dusting of cinnamon, and serve.

If you liked this recipe, you will love these as well.

KUMQUAT chia seed pudding

OATMEAL smoothies

BERRY chia seed pudding

ORANGE FRUIT & VEGGIE smoothies

2	ripe bananas, peeled and cut into 1-inch (2.5-cm) pieces
1	cup (250 ml) freshly squeezed orange juice
1	orange, peeled and cut up into chunks
½	cup (120 ml) unsweetened almond milk
1	carrot, scraped and coarsely chopped
1	fresh orange pepper (capsicum), seeded

Serves 2 • Preparation 10 minutes + 2–12 hours to freeze • Difficulty 1

1. Put the banana pieces in a freezerproof container, cover, and freeze for at least 2 hours. If liked, put them in the freezer the night before.

2. Combine the frozen bananas, orange juice, orange, almond milk, carrot, and pepper in a food processor and chop until smooth.

3. Pour into two glasses, and serve.

GREEN SMOOTHIES with sprouted wheat berries

2   cups (100 g) fresh baby
    spinach leaves

½   cup fresh parsley + extra
    leaves, to garnish

1   small organic cucumber, with
    peel (peel if not organic)

1   large organic Granny Smith
    apple, with peel, cored and
    coarsely chopped

2   kiwifruit, peeled

1   teaspoon finely grated
    unwaxed lime juice

    Freshly squeezed juice
    of 1 lime

1   medium banana, peeled

½   cup (120 ml) low-fat
    (semi-skimmed) milk or
    unsweetened almond milk

2   tablespoons sprouted wheat
    berries

Serves 2 • Preparation 10 minutes • Difficulty 1

1. Combine the spinach, parsley, cucumber, apple, kiwifruit, lime zest and juice, banana, and milk in a food processor and chop until smooth.

2. Pour into two glasses. Place a spoonful of sprouted wheat in each glass. Garnish with parsley, and serve.

KUMQUAT chia seed pudding

Serves 4 • Preparation 10 minutes + 4–12 hours to soak
Difficulty 1

1½	cups (375 ml) unsweetened almond milk	⅓	cup chia seeds
1	cup (250 ml) fat-free or low-fat Greek-style yogurt	1–2	tablespoons maple syrup, or to taste
1	teaspoon vanilla extract (essence)	1	cup (150 g) granola or muesli
		2–4	kumquats, sliced

1. Whisk the almond milk, yogurt, vanilla, chia seeds, and maple syrup in a bowl. Let sit for 5-10 minutes and then whisk again to stop the seeds from clumping.

2. Cover and chill in the refrigerator for 4 hours, or overnight. Stir the mixture once or twice during the chilling time.

3. Stir the mixture well then spoon a layer into the bottom of four serving glasses. Cover with a layer of granola. Spoon in another layer of pudding and granola, and finish with a layer of pudding.

4. Top with the kumquats, and serve.

MUESLI & YOGURT parfait

Serves 4 • Preparation 10 minutes • Difficulty 1

2	cups (500 ml) fat-free or low-fat Greek-style yogurt	1	cup (150 g) fresh blueberries
1	teaspoon vanilla extract (essence)	1	cup (150 g) fresh raspberries
1½	cups (225 g) muesli	4	whole strawberries, to garnish

1. Mix the yogurt and vanilla extract in a bowl.

2. Spoon a layer of the yogurt mixture into four serving glasses or bowls. Cover with a sprinkling each of muesli, blueberries, and raspberries. Repeat until the ingredients are all used up.

3. Garnish each serving with a strawberry, and serve.

OATMEAL smoothies

Serves 2–3 • Preparation 10 minutes • Difficulty 1

2	ripe bananas, peeled	1	cup (150 g) fresh raspberries + extra, to garnish
2	teaspoons ground flaxseed	½	cup (50 g) rolled oats
1	cup (250 ml) reduced-fat (semi-skimmed) milk	2	teaspoons honey
1	cup (250 ml) fat-free or low-fat Greek-style yogurt		

1. Combine the bananas, milk, yogurt, raspberries, rolled oats, and honey in a blender and process until smooth.

2. Pour into two or three serving glasses, garish with the extra raspberries, and serve.

BERRY chia seed pudding

Serves 4–6 • Preparation 10 minutes + 4–12 hours to soak
Cooking 4–5 minutes • Difficulty 1

3	cups (750 ml) unsweetened almond milk	2	cups (300 g) fresh strawberries
½	cup chia seeds		Freshly squeezed juice of 1 lemon
3	tablespoons raw honey		Fresh mint leaves, to garnish

1. Whisk the almond milk, chia seeds, and 2 tablespoons of honey in a bowl. Let sit for 5-10 minutes and then whisk again to stop the seeds from clumping.

2. Cover and chill in the refrigerator for 4 hours, or overnight. Stir the mixture once or twice during the chilling time.

3. About 30 minutes before serving, coarsely chop the strawberries and place in medium saucepan over medium-low heat. Add the remaining tablespoon of honey and the lemon juice and simmer until the strawberries are beginning to soften, 4-5 minutes.

4. Spoon the pudding mixture into four to six serving glasses or bowls. Top with the warm strawberry mixture. Garnish with the mint leaves, and serve.

DRIED FRUIT & NUT muesli bars

2 cups (200 g) rolled oats
1/2 cup (75 g) almonds, coarsely chopped
1/2 cup (75 g) hazelnuts, coarsely chopped
1/2 cup (60 g) pecans, coarsely chopped
1/2 cup (75 g) sunflower seeds
1/4 cup (35 g) pumpkin seeds
1/2 cup (120 ml) honey
1/4 cup (50 g) firmly packed dark brown sugar
2 tablespoons (30 g) butter
1 teaspoon vanilla extract (essence)
1/2 teaspoon sea salt flakes
1/2 cup (60 g) flaked coconut
1/2 cup (90 g) dried apricots, finely chopped
1/3 cup (60 g) dried cranberries, coarsely chopped
1/3 cup (60 g) golden raisins (sultanas)
1/4 cup (25 g) ground flaxseed
1 tablespoon sesame seeds

Serves 16 • Preparation 20 minutes • Cooking 35–45 minutes • Difficulty 1

1. Preheat the oven to 350°F (180°C/gas 4). Grease the base and sides of a 10 x 14-inch (25 x 35-cm) cake pan. Line with parchment paper, extending the paper 2 inches (5 cm) above the rim of the pan.

2. Combine the oats, almonds, hazelnuts, pecans, and sunflower and pumpkin seeds in a large bowl and mix well. Spread out on a large baking sheet and bake, stirring occasionally, for 20–25 minutes, until lightly toasted.

3. Melt the honey, brown sugar, and butter in a small saucepan over low heat. Stir in the vanilla and salt.

4. Combine the coconut, apricots, cranberries, golden raisins, flaxseed, and sesame seeds in a large bowl. Add the toasted oat mixture and stir to combine. Pour in the honey mixture and mix well.

5. Spread in the prepared pan, using the back of a spoon to press down and compact, creating an even surface.

6. Bake for 15–20 minutes, until golden brown. Leave in the pan to cool completely. Cut into sixteen bars to serve.

HOMEMADE MUESLI with yogurt & berries

Muesli

3 cups (300 g) rolled oats

$1/3$ cup (50 g) unsweetened shredded (desiccated) coconut

3 tablespoons pumpkin seeds

3 tablespoons sunflower seeds

2 tablespoons sesame seeds

2 tablespoons poppy seeds

$1/4$ cup (60 ml) extra-virgin rapeseed oil

$1/4$ cup (60 ml) liquid honey

To Serve

1 cup (250 ml) fat-free or low-fat plain Greek-style yogurt

1 cup (150 g) fresh blueberries

$1/4$ cup (60 ml) liquid honey, to drizzle

Serves 8–10 • Preparation 15 minutes + time to cool • Cooking 20–25 minutes • Difficulty 1

Muesli

1. Preheat the oven to 350°F (180°C/gas 4). Line a large shallow baking pan with parchment paper.

2. Mix the rolled oats, coconut, pumpkin seeds, sunflower seeds, and poppy seeds in a large bowl.

3. Combine the rapeseed oil and honey in a small saucepan over medium-low heat. Bring to a gentle simmer.

4. Drizzle the oil and honey mixture over the oat mixture, mixing well. Spread the mixture out in the prepared pan.

5. Bake for 20–25 minutes, stirring occasionally, until crisp and golden. Remove from the oven and let cool completely.

To Serve

1. Spoon the granola into serving bowls. Top with the yogurt, blueberries, and a drizzle of honey, and serve.

These scones are sweetened naturally by the dates. There is just a little raw sugar sprinkled over the top, which adds a delicious gritty texture. They go beautifully with a morning cup of tea or coffee. If there are any leftover, toast them and serve the next day.

DATE & ORANGE scones

2/3	cup (150 ml) milk + extra, to glaze
1	cup (180 g) dried dates, pitted and coarsely chopped
	Finely grated zest of 1 unwaxed orange
1	cup (150 g) all-purpose (plain) flour
1	cup (150 g) whole-wheat (wholemeal) flour
2	teaspoons baking powder
1	teaspoon ground cinnamon
1/2	teaspoon pumpkin pie (mixed) spice
1/8	teaspoon sea salt flakes
1/4	cup (60 g) chilled unsalted butter, diced
	Raw sugar, to sprinkle

Serves 8 • Preparation 15 minutes • Cooking 20–25 minutes
Difficulty 1

1. Preheat the oven to 400°F (200°C/gas 6). Lightly grease a large baking sheet and line with parchment paper.

2. Heat the milk in a small saucepan over medium-low heat until warm. Remove from the heat, add the dates and orange zest, then set aside to cool a little.

3. Sift both flours, baking powder, cinnamon, pumpkin pie spice, and salt into a medium bowl. Add the butter and, using your fingers, rub it into the flour until the mixture resembles coarse crumbs. Make a well in the center and pour in the milk and date mixture. Using a butter knife, stir the flour into the milk mixture until a dough begins to form.

4. Turn out onto a floured work surface and lightly knead to bring the dough together. Do not over work, you want a soft, sticky dough.

5. Shape into an 8-inch (20-cm) round loaf. Place on the prepared baking sheet. Using a sharp knife that has been dipped in flour, mark eight wedges in the top of the dough. Sprinkle with raw sugar.

6. Bake for 20–25 minutes, until golden brown and the base sounds hollow when tapped. Leave on the baking sheet for 10 minutes to cool slightly. Transfer to a wire rack.

7. Serve warm or at room temperature.

DATE & WALNUT muffins

³/₄ cup (120 g) whole-wheat (wholemeal) flour

³/₄ cup (120 g) all-purpose (plain) flour

¹/₃ cup (75 g) firmly packed light brown sugar

1¹/₂ teaspoons pumpkin-pie spice (allspice)

1 teaspoon baking soda (bicarbonate of soda)

¹/₂ teaspoon sea salt flakes

¹/₂ cup (120 ml) reduced fat (semi-skimmed) milk

¹/₃ cup (90 ml) molasses (treacle)

¹/₃ cup (90 ml) light olive, canola, or safflower oil

2 large free-range eggs

1¹/₄ cups (150 g) walnuts, coarsely chopped

1 cup (180 g) pitted dates, coarsely chopped

Serves 12 • Preparation 15 minutes • Cooking 15–20 minutes Difficulty 1

1. Preheat the oven to 400°F (200°C/gas 6). Line a standard 12-cup muffin tin with paper liners.

2. Combine both flours, brown sugar, pumpkin pie spice, baking soda, and salt in a large bowl.

3. Whisk the milk, molasses, oil, and eggs in a separate bowl. Stir into the dry ingredients, mixing until just combined. Stir in the walnuts and dates. Divide the batter evenly among the muffin cups.

4. Bake for 15–20 minutes, until a toothpick inserted into the center of a muffin comes out clean.

5. Leave in the pan for 10 minutes to cool slightly then turn out onto a wire rack.

6. Serve warm or at room temperature.

RHUBARB & PECAN bran muffins

1½ cups (225 g) all-purpose (plain) flour

2 teaspoons baking powder

1 teaspoon ground cinnamon

½ teaspoon baking soda (bicarbonate of soda)

1½ cups (90 g) wheat bran

½ cup (100 g) firmly packed light brown sugar

14 ounces (400 g) rhubarb, about 4 stalks, trimmed and cut into small cubes

½ cup (60 g) pecans, coarsely chopped

1 cup (250 ml) reduced-fat (semi-skimmed) milk

2 large free-range eggs, lightly beaten

¼ cup (60 g) butter, melted and cooled

Serves 10–12 • Preparation 15 minutes • Cooking 20–25 minutes
Difficulty 1

1. Preheat the oven to 400°F (200°C/gas 6). Lightly grease a standard 12-cup muffin pan.

2. Sift the flour, baking powder, cinnamon, and baking soda into a bowl. Stir in the bran and brown sugar. Add the rhubarb and pecans and stir to combine. Pour in the milk, eggs, and butter and mix until just combined. The batter should still be slightly lumpy. Divide the batter evenly among the muffin cups.

3. Bake for 20–25 minutes, until golden brown and a toothpick inserted into the centers comes out clean.

4. Leave in the pan for 10 minutes to cool slightly then turn out onto a wire rack.

5. Serve warm or at room temperature.

Eggs are a nutritious food, packed with high-quality protein, vitamins, and minerals. However, because egg yolks are high in both saturated fats and dietary cholesterol in the past some experts recommended eliminating or restricting them for people with high cholesterol or diabetes. Recent research suggests that eating moderate amounts of eggs (up to four a week), may actually help prevent Type 2 diabetes. If preferred, you can make the egg dishes on this page and the next pages using egg whites only. This will reduce the amount of dietary cholesterol and saturated fat.

MEXICAN EGGS & BEANS with avocado

3	ounces (90 g) soft, fresh Mexican chorizo, diced
1	medium red bell pepper (capsicum), chopped
1	jalapeño pepper, chopped (remove seeds for less heat)
1	(14-ounce/400-g) can pinto beans, drained and rinsed
4	scallions (spring onions), sliced
6	large eggs + 2 large egg whites
1/4	cup (60 ml) water
	Freshly ground sea salt and black pepper
1	cup crushed baked tortilla chips
1/2	cup (60 g) shredded low-fat cheddar cheese
1/2	cup chopped fresh cilantro (coriander)
1	avocado, pitted, peeled and sliced
2	tablespoons low-fat sour cream

Serves 4–6 • Preparation 15 minutes • Cooking 15 minutes
Difficulty 1

1. Dry-fry the chorizo in a large frying pan over medium heat until it just begins to brown, about 3 minutes. Add the bell pepper and jalapeño and cook, stirring occasionally, until they begin to sizzle, about 5 minutes.

2. Add the beans and half of the scallions and cook, stirring occasionally, until heated through, about 4 minutes.

3. Whisk the whole eggs and egg whites with the water in a bowl. Season with salt and pepper. Add to the pan and cook, stirring, until just beginning to set, about 2 minutes.

4. Add the tortilla chips, cheese, half of the cilantro, and the remaining scallions and continue cooking and stirring until the eggs are just set, 3–4 minutes.

5. Divide the egg mixture among four to six serving plates. Top with the avocado, sour cream, and remaining cilantro, and serve hot.

If you liked this recipe, you will love these as well.

BROCCOLI & PEA FRITTATA
with goat cheese

ZUCCHINI
hashed browns

FREE-RANGE EGG
& FRESH HERB salad

BROCCOLI & PEA FRITTATA with goat cheese

2 cups (300 g) frozen peas

1 small broccoli, cut into small florets

6 large free-range eggs

2 tablespoons crème fraîche

3 tablespoons finely chopped fresh parsley

1 tablespoon finely chopped fresh mint

1 tablespoon freshly grated Parmesan cheese

4 ounces (120 g) goat cheese, crumbled or grated

Freshly ground sea salt and black pepper

1 tablespoon extra-virgin olive oil

4 scallions (spring onions), thinly sliced

Fresh salad greens, to serve

Serves 4 • Preparation 15 minutes • Cooking 12–15 minutes Difficulty 1

1. Cook the peas and broccoli in a pan of boiling water for 2 minutes. Drain and pat dry.

2. Preheat an overhead broiler (grill) on medium-high.

3. Whisk the eggs in a bowl and with the crème fraîche. Stir in the parsley, mint, Parmesan, and almost all the goat cheese (leave a little to garnish). Season with salt and pepper.

4. Heat the oil in a 10-inch (25-cm) frying pan with an ovenproof handle and sauté the scallions with the broccoli and peas until softened, 3–4 minutes. Pour in the egg mixture, stirring gently. Cook over medium heat without stirring, until the egg is beginning to set but still moist on top and the base is lightly golden, for 3–4 minutes.

5. Garnish with the remaining goat cheese and place the pan under the broiler. Cook for 4–5 minutes, until set. Serve warm with the salad greens.

ZUCCHINI hashed browns

2   cups (400 g) coarsely grated zucchini (courgettes)

4   large free-range eggs, beaten

1   small white onion, finely chopped

1   clove garlic, finely chopped

1   tablespoon finely chopped fresh parsley

    Freshly ground sea salt and black pepper

2   tablespoons extra-virgin olive oil

    Tomato ketchup, to serve

Serves 2 • Preparation 10 minutes • Cooking 20 minutes • Difficulty 1

1. Combine the zucchini, eggs, onion, garlic, and parsley in a large bowl. Season with salt and pepper and mix well.

2. Heat 1 tablespoon of oil in a large frying pan over medium-high heat. Add half the zucchini mixture, spreading it to an even thickness. Cook until browned, then flip and cook the other side, about 5 minutes each side.

3. Slice onto a plate. Cook the remaining zucchini mixture in the same way.

4. Serve warm, with the ketchup.

appetizers & snacks

OAT crackers

1½ cups (150 g) rolled oats
+ extra, to sprinkle

1½ cups (225 g) whole-wheat
(wholemeal) flour

2 teaspoons sea salt flakes
+ extra, to sprinkle

1 teaspoon superfine (caster)
sugar

1 teaspoon baking powder

½ cup (120 g) chilled unsalted
butter, diced

⅓ cup (90 ml) ice water

Makes 40 crackers • Preparation 20 minutes + 30 minutes to chill
Cooking 15 minutes • Difficulty 1

1. Put the oats in a food processor and blend until coarsely chopped. Add the whole-wheat flour, salt, sugar, and baking powder and blend to combine. Add the butter and blend until the mixture resembles coarse crumbs. Pour in the water and blend until a dough begins to form.

2. Turn out onto a clean work surface and knead to combine. Divide the dough in half and shape into two disks. Wrap in plastic wrap (cling film) and refrigerate for 30 minutes.

3. Preheat the oven to 350°F (180°C/gas 4). Grease two large baking sheets and line with parchment paper.

4. Roll one piece of dough out between two sheets of parchment paper to about ¼ inch (5 mm) thick to make an 8 x 10-inch (20 x 25-cm) rectangle. Trim the edges to straighten. Cut the dough in half lengthwise and then into five crosswise, to make ten rectangles. Cut each rectangle in half diagonally to make twenty triangles. Repeat with the remaining dough.

5. Place the crackers about ¾ inch (2 cm) apart on the prepared baking sheets. Sprinkle with extra oats and salt.

6. Bake for 15 minutes, until crisp and pale golden brown. Rotate the baking sheets halfway through for even baking.

7. Let the crackers cool on the baking sheets for 2–3 minutes, until they are firm enough to move. Transfer to a wire rack and let cool completely.

The crackers on this page and the previous one are both good alternatives to commercially produced crackers which often contain unhealthy ingredients, including trans fats. Decades of research shows that consuming trans fats, also known as partially hydrogenated oil, is strongly linked to heart disease and obesity. Food companies use partially hydrogenated oils as a cheaper alternative to butter and lard.

MULTIGRAIN crackers

$1/2$ cup (75 g) whole-wheat (wholemeal) flour
$1/4$ cup (30 g) all-purpose (plain) flour
$1/4$ cup (30 g) gram (besan) flour
$1/4$ cup (20 g) fine polenta
1 tablespoon ground flaxseed
2 teaspoons sea salt flakes
1 teaspoon ground cumin
1 teaspoon ground coriander
1 teaspoon sweet paprika
$1/3$ cup (90 ml) water
$1/4$ cup (60 ml) extra-virgin olive oil
1 tablespoon honey
2 tablespoons sunflower seeds
2 tablespoons pumpkin seeds
2 tablespoons sesame seeds
1 tablespoon poppy seeds

Makes 20 crackers • Preparation 15 minutes + 30 minutes to chill Cooking 20–25 minutes • Difficulty 1

1. Combine all three flours with the polenta, flaxseed, salt, cumin, coriander, and paprika in a food processor and blend to combine.

2. Combine the water, oil, and honey in a small bowl. With the motor running, gradually add the liquid to the flour mixture and pulse to combine. Transfer to a bowl, add the sunflower, pumpkin, sesame, and poppy seeds and stir and knead to combine.

3. Divide the dough in half and shape into two disks. Wrap in plastic wrap (cling film) and refrigerate for 30 minutes.

4. Preheat the oven to 350°F (180°C/gas 4). Lightly grease two large baking sheets.

5. Roll the dough out between two sheets of parchment paper to about $1/4$ inch (5 mm) thick to make an 8 x 10-inch (20 x 25-cm) rectangle. Trim the edges to straighten. Cut the dough in half lengthwise and then into five crosswise, to make ten rectangles.

6. Place about $3/4$ inch (2 cm) apart on the prepared baking sheets. Repeat with the remaining dough.

7. Bake for 20–25 minutes, until crisp and golden brown. Rotate the baking sheets halfway through for even baking.

8. Let the crackers cool on the baking sheets for 2–3 minutes, until they are firm enough to move. Transfer to a wire rack and let cool completely.

TZATZIKI

1	Lebanese or ordinary cucumber
$1/2$	teaspoon sea salt flakes
$1\frac{1}{2}$	cups (375 g) fat-free or low-fat Greek-style plain yogurt
1	tablespoon freshly squeezed lemon juice
1	tablespoon extra-virgin olive oil
1	tablespoon finely chopped fresh mint
1	clove garlic, minced
	Carrot sticks, to serve
	Celery stalks, to serve
	Florets of raw cauliflower and broccoli, to serve

Serves 8 • Preparation 15 minutes + 20 minutes to drain • Difficulty 1

1. Peel the cucumber. Cut in half lengthwise and, using a teaspoon, scrape out and discard the seeds. Coarsely grate the flesh.

2. Place the cucumber flesh in a sieve or colander, sprinkle with the salt, and set over a bowl to drain for 20 minutes.

3. Squeeze out any remaining liquid from the cucumber using your hands. Transfer the flesh to a medium bowl. Add the yogurt, lemon juice, oil, mint, and garlic and stir to combine.

4. Serve immediately with the vegetables.

FRESH PEA hummus

3	whole-wheat (wholemeal) pita breads, to serve
2	cups (300 g) fresh shelled green peas
1	(14-ounce/400-g) can garbanzo beans (chickpeas), drained and rinsed
$^1/_2$	cup chopped fresh parsley
1	clove garlic
$^1/_3$	cup (90 ml) fat-free or low-fat Greek-style plain yogurt
3	scallions (spring onions), trimmed and coarsely chopped
3	tablespoons freshly squeezed lemon juice
1	teaspoon ground cumin
1	teaspoon sea salt flakes
2	tablespoons extra-virgin olive oil

Serves 6 • Preparation 15 minutes • Cooking 10 minutes • Difficulty 1

1. Preheat the oven to 350°F (180°C/gas 6). Cut or tear the pita breads into 6–8 triangles each. Place in a single layer on a large rimmed baking sheet. Bake for 10 minutes, until crisp and golden brown.

2. While the pita breads are toasting, chop the green peas, garbanzo beans, parsley, garlic, yogurt, scallions, lemon juice, cumin, and salt in a food processor until almost smooth. Don't overprocess; leave a little bit of texture.

3. Place the hummus in a serving bowl and drizzle with the oil. Serve with the warm toasted pita breads.

This dish makes an elegant appetizer or snack. For best results, choose very fresh, high-quality wild salmon. If you ask your fishmonger to clean and thinly slice the salmon the dish can be prepared in just a few minutes.

SALMON CARPACCIO with thyme & lemon

1	teaspoon coarse sea salt
2	tablespoons brine-cured green peppercorns, drained
1-2	teaspoons fresh thyme leaves
6	tablespoons (90 ml) extra-virgin olive oil
	Freshly squeezed juice of 1 lemon
1	pound (500 g) very fresh salmon fillet, thinly sliced
1	lemon, cut into wedges, to garnish

Serves 8-12 • Preparation 15 minutes + 4 hours to chill • Difficulty 1

1. Coarsely pound the salt and half the peppercorns with a mortar and pestle. Add the thyme and mix well.

2. Whisk 4 tablespoons of the oil with the lemon juice and salt mixture in a small bowl.

3. Arrange the salmon on a large serving dish and pour the dressing over the top. Cover with plastic wrap (cling film) and chill in the refrigerator for 4 hours.

4. Remove the plastic wrap and drizzle with the remaining oil. Garnish with the remaining peppercorns and the lemon wedges, and serve.

If you liked this recipe, you will love these as well.

SCALLOP skewers

CEVICHE

VIETNAMESE SHRIMP rolls

ROASTED BELL PEPPERS with anchovies

2   yellow bell peppers (capsicums)

2   green bell peppers (capsicums)

2   red bell peppers (capsicums)

8   anchovy fillets

4   cloves garlic, finely chopped

4   tablespoons finely chopped fresh parsley

2   tablespoons brine-cured capers, drained

$1/2$ teaspoon dried oregano

4   tablespoons (60 ml) extra-virgin olive oil

2   tablespoons coarsely chopped fresh basil leaves

Serves 6–8 • Preparation 15 minutes + $2^{1}/_{4}$ hours to sweat & marinate
Cooking 20–30 minutes • Difficulty 1

1. Preheat the oven to 400°F (200°C/gas 6). Slice the bell peppers in half lengthwise. Remove the seeds and pulpy core. Rinse under cold running water and shake dry.

2. Bake in the oven, skin-side up, until the skins are blistered and black, 20–30 minutes. Place in a plastic bag and leave to sweat for 15 minutes.

3. Remove the charred skins from the bell peppers with your fingers. Cut into strips about 2 inches (5 cm) wide.

4. Crumble the anchovy fillets in a small bowl and add the garlic, parsley, capers, oregano, oil, and basil.

5. Place half the bell peppers in a large serving dish. Drizzle with half the anchovy mixture. Cover with the remaining bell peppers and anchovy mixture.

6. Set aside to marinate for 2 hours before serving.

CHEESE & CELERY *snacks*

8	ounces (250 g) fresh ricotta cheese, drained
4	ounces (125 g) blue cheese, crumbled into small pieces
$\frac{1}{4}$	cup (60 g) milk or sour cream
2	cloves garlic, finely chopped
1	tablespoon finely chopped fresh chives
1	tablespoon extra-virgin olive oil
	Freshly ground sea salt and black pepper
12	large stalks very fresh celery
1	tablespoon finely chopped fresh parsley

Serves 12 • Preparation 15 minutes + 1 hour to chill • Difficulty 1

1. Put the ricotta in a bowl. Add the blue cheese and milk and mash until smooth and creamy. Add the garlic, chives, oil, salt, and pepper, mixing well.

2. Cover and chill in the refrigerator for 1 hour.

3. Trim the celery stalks and remove any tough external fibers. Cut into pieces about 3 inches (8 cm) long.

4. Fill the celery with the cheese mixture, sprinkle with the parsley, and serve.

SCALLOP skewers

Serves 6 • Preparation 15 minutes • Cooking 5 minutes
Difficulty 2

1	(1-inch/2.5-cm) piece fresh ginger, peeled Small bunch fresh cilantro (coriander)	20	small to medium scallops, shucked Sweet chili sauce, to serve
2	cloves garlic, peeled		
6	tablespoons (90 ml) extra-virgin olive oil		

1. Combine the ginger, cilantro, and garlic in a mortar and pound with the pestle to make a paste.

2. Add 4 tablespoons of oil, mixing well. Pour over the scallops and stir until evenly coated. Thread each scallop onto a short wooden skewer.

3. Heat the remaining 2 tablespoons of oil in a medium frying pan until very hot.

4. Place 4–6 skewers in the pan and cook for 2 minutes, until just golden. Turn over, and cook until golden on the other side. Set aside in a warm oven while you cook the remaining skewers.

5. Serve the scallops warm, with sweet chili sauce.

TOMATO & CHEESE skewers

Serves 10 • Preparation 15 minutes • Difficulty 1

40	cherry tomatoes		Extra-virgin olive oil, to drizzle
20	bocconcini (small balls of mozzarella cheese)		Freshly ground sea salt and black pepper
20	leaves fresh basil		

1. Break ten long thin bamboo skewers in half. Thread each one with a cherry tomato, followed by a ball of mozzarella, a basil leaf, and another tomato.

2. Repeat until you have used up all the ingredients to make 20 skewers.

3. Arrange the skewers on serving platters. Season with salt and pepper, drizzle with oil, and serve.

HONEYED CHICKEN skewers

Serves 12 • Preparation 15 minutes + 2 hours to marinate
Cooking 15–20 minutes • Difficulty 1

2	red chilies, minced	2	teaspoons soy sauce
6	scallions (spring onions), thinly sliced	2	pounds (1 kg) chicken breast fillets, trimmed, cut into small cubes
4	cloves garlic, minced		
1	(1-inch/2.5-cm) piece ginger, finely grated	2	tablespoons white sesame seeds, toasted
3/4	cup (180 ml) honey Freshly squeezed juice of 3 lemons		Zest of 1 unwaxed lemon, grated or in thin strips, to serve

1. Combine the chilies, scallions, garlic, ginger, honey, lemon juice, and soy in a bowl. Thread the chicken onto small metal or wooden skewers, 4–5 pieces on each skewer. Place in a shallow dish. Pour in the marinade. Cover and chill for at least 2 hours.

2. Preheat the oven to 300°F (150°C/gas 2). Line two baking sheets with parchment paper.

3. Preheat a lightly oiled grill pan (griddle) over medium-high heat. Grill the skewers in batches, turning often, until cooked through and golden, 6–8 minutes each batch.

4. Place the cooked skewers on the prepared baking sheets and keep warm in the oven while you cook the remaining skewers. Serve hot.

CHICKEN MEATBALL skewers

Serves 6–12 • Preparation 15 minutes • Cooking 30–35 minutes • Difficulty 1

1	pound (500 g) ground (minced) chicken	1/2	teaspoon ground cumin
1	onion, finely chopped	1/4	teaspoon black pepper
3	cloves garlic, minced	1/2	cup (75 g) fine dry bread crumbs
2	tablespoons chopped cilantro (coriander)	1	large egg
1	teaspoon garam masala	1	teaspoon sea salt flakes
1	teaspoon hot chili powder	12	bocconcini (mozzarella cherry balls)
1/4	teaspoon turmeric	12	cherry tomatoes
		12	fresh basil leaves

1. Preheat the oven to 350°F (180°C/gas 4). Line a large baking sheet with aluminum foil.

2. Combine the chicken, onion, garlic, cilantro, garam masala, chili powder, turmeric, cumin, pepper, bread crumbs, egg, and salt in a bowl. Stir to combine.

3. Brush your hands with oil. Divide the chicken mixture into 12 equal portions and roll into balls. Arrange on the prepared baking sheet.

4. Bake for 30–35 minutes, until cooked through. Turn on the broiler (grill) at the top of the oven and broil (grill) until crisp and golden, turning a few times.

5. Thread the meatballs onto 12 skewers, alternating with the tomatoes, cheese, and basil. Serve warm.

CEVICHE

1½ pounds (750 g) firm skinless fish fillets (such as mackerel, halibut, tuna, sea bass), boned and thinly sliced

Freshly squeezed juice of 6 limes

Freshly squeezed juice of 2 lemons

2 medium tomatoes, diced

1 small red onion, halved and thinly sliced

1 avocado, pitted and diced

½ cup coarsely chopped fresh cilantro (coriander) + extra, to garnish

2 small green chilies, seeded and thinly sliced

2 tablespoons extra-virgin olive oil

Freshly ground sea salt and black pepper

Serves 8 • Preparation 15 minutes + 4 hours to marinate • Difficulty 1

1. Combine the fish and lime and lemon juice in a medium glass or stainless steel bowl. Cover and refrigerate, stirring occasionally, until the fish turns from opaque to white, about 4 hours.

2. Drain the fish, reserving 3 tablespoons of the marinade. Combine the fish, tomatoes, onion, avocado, cilantro, and chilies on a serving platter.

3. Whisk the reserved marinade and oil in a small bowl. Season with salt and pepper. Drizzle over the fish, tossing gently to coat.

4. Garnish with the cilantro, and serve.

VIETNAMESE SHRIMP rolls

Sweet Chili Dipping Sauce

1	cup (250 ml) rice vinegar
$1/4$	cup (60 ml) water
4	tablespoons sugar
1	red chile, finely chopped
2	teaspoons salt
1	clove garlic, minced

Shrimp Rolls

3	ounces (90 g) vermicelli rice noodles
12	rice paper sheets (wrappers)
6	butter lettuce or other soft lettuce leaves
$1/2$	cup fresh mint
$1/2$	cup fresh cilantro (coriander)
1	red bell pepper (capsicum) seeded and thinly sliced lengthwise
1	cup (50 g) bean sprouts
8	cooked shrimp (prawns), peeled and halved lengthwise

Serves 4-6 • Preparation 30 minutes • Cooking 10 minutes • Difficulty 2

Sweet Chili Dipping Sauce

1. Combine all the sauce ingredients in a small saucepan and simmer over low heat until the sugar has dissolved and the liquid is slightly syrupy, 5-7 minutes. Set aside to cool.

Shrimp Rolls

1. Place the noodles in a bowl, cover with hot water and soak until soft, 2-3 minutes. Drain and chop into short lengths.

2. Soak the rice papers one at a time in a bowl of warm water until soft, about 30 seconds. Lay on a damp kitchen towel.

3. Place half a lettuce leaf and 1-2 tablespoons of noodles just below the center of the rice paper, allowing enough space at the sides to fold over. Lay a few mint and cilantro leaves, a little bell pepper and bean sprouts, and 2 shrimp halves on top. Fold the base and the sides of the rice paper over the filling and roll until firmly enclosed. Repeat with the remaining wrappers and filling.

4. Serve with the dipping sauce.

You will need sugarcane sticks to make these tasty appetizers. If you can't get them, use cake pop or ice lolly sticks.

CHICKEN STICKS with sweet chili sauce

1	pound (500 g) ground (minced) chicken
3	scallions (spring onions), white part only, finely chopped
2	tablespoons Thai fish sauce
2	tablespoons freshly squeezed lime juice
1	large free-range egg white
2	cloves garlic, finely chopped
2	teaspoons peeled and finely grated ginger
$1/2$	teaspoon sea salt flakes
2	tablespoons finely chopped fresh cilantro (coriander) leaves
12	(6-inch/15-cm) sugarcane sticks
	Sweet chili sauce, to serve

Serves 6 • Preparation 20 minutes + 30 minutes to marinate • Cooking 8–10 minutes • Difficulty 1

1. Combine the chicken, scallions, fish sauce, lime juice, egg white, garlic, ginger, and salt in a food processor and pulse to combine. Transfer to a bowl, add the cilantro, mixing well.

2. Divide the mixture into twelve equal-size portions. Using wet hands, shape the mixture around the lower two-thirds of each sugarcane stick. Place on a platter, cover, and refrigerate for 30 minutes.

3. Preheat an indoor grill to medium heat or prepare a medium fire in an outdoor grill. Brush the grill with oil.

4. Grill the sticks, turning occasionally, until just cooked through and golden brown, 8–10 minutes.

5. Transfer to a serving plate and serve hot, with the sweet chili sauce for dipping.

If you liked this recipe, you will love these as well.

TOMATO & CHEESE
skewers

HONEYED CHICKEN
skewers

CHICKEN MEATBALL
skewers

soups & salads

GAZPACHO

6	large slices day-old, firm-textured bread, crusts removed
3	pounds (1.5 kg) ripe, fresh tomatoes
2	cucumbers, peeled, halved, and seeded
1	red bell pepper (capsicum), halved, seeded
1	red onion, halved
1	clove garlic
6	tablespoons (90 ml) extra-virgin olive oil
1	tablespoon sherry vinegar
1	tablespoon freshly squeezed lemon juice
$1/4$	teaspoon ground cumin
	Freshly ground sea salt and black pepper
2	stalks celery, with leaves attached
1	cup (120 g) blanched whole almonds, split

Serves 6 • Preparation 20 minutes + 2–3 hours to chill • Cooking 5 minutes • Difficulty 1

1. Cut two slices of the bread into small cubes and set aside. Soak the remaining four slices of bread in a bowl of water for 10 minutes. Squeeze out the excess water and set aside.

2. Cut a cross in the base of each tomato. Blanch in a pan of boiling water for 10 seconds. Let cool for a few minutes, then slip off the skins. Chop coarsely.

3. Coarsely chop one of the cucumbers, half the bell pepper, and half the onion, and add to the tomatoes.

4. Process the soaked bread and garlic in a food processor until a paste forms. Add the tomatoes and coarsely chopped vegetables and process until smooth.

5. With the motor running, gradually add 4 tablespoons (60 ml) of oil, the vinegar, lemon juice, and cumin. Season with salt and pepper. Chill for at least 2–3 hours, or until ready to serve.

6. When ready to serve, finely chop the celery, and the remaining cucumber, bell pepper, and onion, keeping them all separate.

7. Heat a small frying pan over medium heat. Add the almonds and cook, shaking the pan often, until golden.

8. Heat the remaining oil in the same frying pan over medium heat. Add the bread cubes and cook, tossing, until golden.

9. Serve the gazpacho chilled, sprinkled with the chopped vegetables, fried bread, and almonds.

Cool, crisp cucumber and thick Greek-style yogurt are both low in carbohydrates, making this soup an ideal choice for diabetics. Greek-style yogurt, in its plain, nonfat, and low-fat forms, is strained to remove much of the liquid whey, lactose, and sugar, giving it its thick consistency and removing many of the carbs and sugars found in regular yogurt. Greek yogurt is also a better source of protein: a typical 6-ounce (180-g) serving contains 15 to 20 grams (the amount in 2–3 ounces (60–90 g) of lean meat). An identical serving of regular yogurt provides just 9 grams of protein.

CHILLED CUCUMBER SOUP with garlic shrimp

Soup

$2^1/_2$	large cucumbers, peeled
$1^1/_4$	cups (300 ml) plain, thick Greek-style yogurt
$^1/_3$	cup (90 ml) crème fraîche
$1^1/_4$	cups (300 ml) chicken stock
	Few drops Tabasco sauce
1	teaspoon salt
2	tablespoons chopped fresh mint
2	tablespoons chopped fresh chives
2	tablespoons chopped fresh dill

Garlic Shrimp

$^1/_4$	cup (60 ml) extra-virgin olive oil
14	ounces (400 g) medium shrimp (prawns), peeled, tails on
4	cloves garlic, sliced
1	small red chili, seeded and thinly sliced
	Sea salt flakes
1	cup (50 g) coarsely chopped fresh parsley

Serves 4 • Preparation 20 minutes + 4–12 hours to chill • Cooking 2–3 minutes • Difficulty 1

Soup

1. Cut two cucumbers in half and scrape out the seeds. Chop in a food processor with the yogurt, crème fraîche, chicken stock, Tabasco, salt, mint, chives, and dill until smooth.

2. Place in a bowl, cover, and chill in the coldest part of the refrigerator for at least 4 hours, or overnight.

3. Use a vegetable peeler to cut long strips from the remaining half cucumber. Cover and chill.

Garlic Shrimp

1. Heat the oil in a frying pan over medium-high heat. Add the shrimp, garlic, and chili and sauté until the shrimp are cooked through, 2–3 minutes. Season with salt. Add the parsley and toss gently. Let cool to room temperature.

2. Ladle the soup into four serving bowls. Put the shrimp in the center of each bowl. Top with the cucumber, and serve.

If you liked this recipe, you will love these as well.

VIETNAMESE SHRIMP rolls

GAZPACHO

TOMATO SOUP with garlic croutons

TOMATO SOUP with garlic croutons

Soup

2	tablespoons extra-virgin olive oil
3¹/₂	ounces (100 g) bacon, finely chopped
1	onion, finely chopped
3	stalks celery, finely chopped
2	carrots, finely chopped
2	cloves garlic, finely chopped
¹/₃	teaspoon red pepper flakes
2	(14-ounce/400-g) cans tomatoes, with juice
2	cups (500 ml) water

Croutons

4	cloves garlic, finely chopped
2	tablespoons extra-virgin olive oil
3	large thick slices granary bread, cut into cubes
	Fresh basil, to serve

Serves 4–6 • Preparation 20 minutes • Cooking 30–35 minutes
Difficulty 1

Soup

1. Heat the oil in a large soup pot over medium heat. Add the bacon, onion, celery, and carrots and sauté until softened, about 5 minutes. Add the garlic and red pepper flakes and sauté until aromatic, about 1 minute.

2. Add the tomatoes and water. Bring to a boil then simmer on low heat, stirring occasionally, for about 25 minutes.

Croutons

1. While the soup is simmering, preheat the oven to 400°F (200°C/gas 6). Combine the garlic and oil in a bowl. Add the bread and toss to coat. Place on a baking sheet and bake for 10 minutes, until crisp and golden brown.

2. Remove the soup from the heat and purée in a food processor or using a handheld blender.

3. Return the soup to low heat and simmer, stirring, until heated through, 2–3 minutes. Ladle into serving bowls. Serve hot, garnished with the croutons and basil.

SWEET POTATO soup

2   tablespoons extra-virgin olive oil

1   large onion, coarsely chopped

2   cloves garlic, finely chopped

2   teaspoons finely grated fresh ginger

2   teaspoons ground cumin

2   pounds (1 kg) sweet potatoes, peeled and coarsely chopped

4   cups (1 liter) vegetable or chicken stock

     Freshly ground sea salt and black pepper

$^1/_2$ cup (120 ml) far-free or low-fat Greek-style plain yogurt

     Chopped fresh chives, to serve

Serves 6 • Preparation 20 minutes • Cooking 20–25 minutes
Difficulty 1

1. Heat the oil in a large soup pot over medium heat. Add the onion and sauté until softened, 3–4 minutes. Add the garlic, ginger, and cumin. Sauté until aromatic, 1–2 minutes.

2. Add the sweet potatoes and vegetable or chicken stock. Increase the heat to high and bring to a boil. Cover and reduce the heat to low. Simmer until the vegetables are soft, 15–20 minutes.

3. Remove from the heat and purée in a food processor or using a handheld blender.

4. Return the soup to low heat and stir until heated through. Season with salt and pepper. Ladle into serving bowls. Top each bowl with a dollop of yogurt and some chives, and serve hot.

44

Tomatoes are one of the non-starchy vegetables that a diabetic can eat more of to satisfy his or her appetite. Like other non-starchy vegetables and fruits, tomatoes have a low glycemic index. They are also rich in lycopene, an antioxidant that may reduce the risk of cancer (especially prostate cancer), heart disease, and macular degeneration. Enjoy them raw or cooked—they are nutritious in both states.

SPICY TOMATO & BEAN soup

4	cloves garlic, chopped
1	teaspoon red pepper flakes, or to taste + extra, to serve
1	teaspoon coriander
$3/4$	teaspoon sea salt flakes
$1/8$	teaspoon caraway seeds
2	tablespoons extra-virgin olive oil
1	(14-ounce/400-g) can garbanzo beans (chickpeas), drained and rinsed
1	(14-ounce/400-g) can tomatoes, with juice
4	cups (1 liter) chicken stock
	Fresh basil, to garnish
	Plain Greek-style yogurt, to serve

Serves 4–6 • Preparation 20 minutes • Cooking 20 minutes
Difficulty 1

1. Crush the garlic, red pepper flakes, coriander, salt, and caraway seeds with a pestle and mortar or spice grinder to form a paste.

2. Heat the oil in a soup pot over medium heat. Add the garlic mixture, and sauté until fragrant, 1–2 minutes.

3. Stir in the garbanzo beans, tomatoes, and chicken stock. Bring to a boil, then simmer, stirring often, for 15 minutes. Let cool slightly.

4. Remove from the heat and purée in a food processor or using a handheld blender.

5. Return to medium-low heat and stir until warmed through. Ladle into serving bowls. Garnish with the basil and yogurt and serve hot with extra red pepper flakes in a small bowl passed separately.

If you liked this recipe, you will love these as well.

GAZPACHO

TOMATO SOUP
with garlic croutons

AZTEC CHICKEN
soup

MINTY PEA soup

Serves 4–6 • Preparation 15 minutes • Cooking 20 minutes
Difficulty 1

2	ounces (60 g) of cubed pancetta	4	cups (600 g) frozen peas
2	medium potatoes, peeled and chopped		Small bunch fresh mint, chopped
4	cups (1 liter) chicken stock		

1. Dry-fry the pancetta in a soup pot over medium heat until crisp and golden brown, 4–5 minutes. Scoop out the pancetta and set aside as a garnish.

2. Add the potatoes and chicken stock to the pot and simmer until the potatoes are tender, about 10 minutes. Add the peas and simmer for 5 minutes. Stir in the mint.

3. Remove from the heat and purée using a handheld blender or in a food processor.

4. Ladle into serving bowls. Garnish with the reserved pancetta, and serve hot.

MUSHROOM SOUP with kasha

Serves 4 • Preparation 25 minutes • Cooking 30 minutes
Difficulty 1

2	tablespoons extra-virgin olive oil	4	ounces (120 g) kasha (buckwheat groats)
1	medium onion, finely chopped	1	bay leaf
6	ounces (180 g) mixed wild mushrooms, thinly sliced	5	cups (1.25 liters) water
			Freshly ground sea salt and black pepper
2	cloves garlic, minced	1	tablespoon fresh thyme leaves, to garnish

1. Heat the oil in a soup pot over medium heat. Add the onion and sauté until softened, 3–4 minutes. Stir in the mushrooms and garlic. Sauté until the mushrooms have softened slightly, about 5 minutes.

2. Add the kasha and bay leaf. Pour in the water. Bring to a boil, lower the heat, and simmer until the kasha is tender and the mushrooms are cooked, about 20 minutes. Remove the bay leaf.

3. Season with salt and pepper. Garnish with the thyme. Serve hot.

ADUKI BEAN soup

Serves 6 • Preparation 20 minutes + 12 hours to soak
Cooking 1½ hours • Difficulty 1

¼	cup (60 ml) sunflower oil		chicken stock
2	onions, finely chopped	1½	cups (200 g) dried aduki beans, soaked overnight
2	stalks celery, finely chopped	1	(14-ounce/400-g) can tomatoes, with juice
3	carrots, finely chopped	1	tablespoon tomato paste (concentrate)
2	cloves garlic, finely chopped		Freshly ground sea salt and black pepper
1	tablespoon finely chopped fresh thyme	2	tablespoons finely chopped fresh parsley
2	bay leaves		
7	cups (1.75 liters)		

1. Heat the oil in a large soup pot over medium heat. Add the onions, celery, carrots, garlic, thyme, and bay leaves and sauté until the onion is softened, about 5 minutes.

2. Pour in the chicken stock and add the aduki beans. Bring to a boil and simmer over low heat until the beans are tender, about 1 hour.

3. Stir in the tomatoes and tomato paste and simmer for 20 minutes. Remove the bay leaves. Season with salt and pepper and stir in 1 tablespoon of the parsley.

4. Serve hot, garnished with the remaining parsley.

LENTIL SOUP with veggies

Serves 4–6 • Preparation 15 minutes • Cooking 30–40 minutes • Difficulty 1

1½	cups (300 g) dried red lentils	3	finely chopped fresh sage leaves
1	onion, finely chopped	2	tablespoons finely chopped fresh rosemary
2	small carrots, diced		Freshly ground sea salt and black pepper
2	stalks celery, thinly sliced		
1	bay leaf	2	tablespoons extra-virgin olive oil
2	cloves garlic, finely chopped		
	Water		

1. Combine the lentils in a soup pot with the onion, carrots, celery, bay leaf, and garlic. Add enough cold water to cover by about 2 inches (5 cm). Cover the pot and simmer over low heat until the lentils are tender, 20–25 minutes.

2. Discard the bay leaf, add the sage and rosemary, and continue cooking, still covered and over low heat, for 10–15 minutes. At this point the lentils should be very soft and will begin to disintegrate.

3. Season with salt and pepper to taste, drizzle with the oil, and serve hot.

AZTEC CHICKEN soup

2	boneless skinless chicken breasts
1	chicken stock cube
4	cups (1 liter) water
2	tablespoons extra-virgin olive oil
1	red onion, finely chopped
1	tablespoon ground cumin
1	teaspoon chili powder
1	(14-ounce/400-g) can tomatoes, with juice
1	(14-ounce/400-g) can red kidney beans, drained and rinsed
	Freshly ground sea salt and black pepper
1	large avocado, halved, peeled, coarsely chopped
1	(14-ounce/400-g) can corn (sweetcorn) kernels, drained and rinsed
1/2	cup coarsely chopped fresh cilantro (coriander)
1	tablespoon freshly squeezed lime juice

Serves 4-6 • Preparation 15 minutes • Cooking 25–30 minutes
Difficulty 1

1. Put the chicken and stock cube in a saucepan and cover with the water. Bring to a boil, then simmer on low until the chicken is cooked through, 8–10 minutes. Use tongs to transfer the chicken to a plate. Reserve the cooking liquid. Let the chicken cool slightly, then shred.

2. Heat the oil in a soup pot over medium heat. Add the onion and sauté until softened, 3–4 minutes. Add the cumin and chili and stir for 30 seconds. Add the reserved cooking liquid and tomatoes and bring to a boil.

3. Add the shredded chicken and kidney beans. Return to a boil then simmer, stirring occasionally, until thickened, about 10 minutes. Season with salt and pepper.

4. Meanwhile, combine the avocado, corn, cilantro, and lime juice in a small bowl.

5. Ladle the soup into serving bowls. Top with spoonfuls of the avocado mixture, and serve hot.

MEXICAN BEAN SOUP with salsa garnish

Soup

1	pound (500 g) pinto beans, or mixed dried beans
3	tablespoons vegetable oil
2	onions, coarsely chopped
2	large carrots, chopped
2	stalks celery, chopped
3	cloves garlic, finely chopped
	Bouquet garni of parsley sprigs, thyme sprigs, 2 bay leaves, rosemary sprig
4	ounces (120 g) pancetta or bacon, diced
2	(14-ounce/400-g) cans tomatoes, with juice
1	tablespoon cumin seeds
1	tablespoon dried oregano
	Freshly ground sea salt and black pepper
$1/4$	cup (60 ml) dry sherry
	Freshly squeezed juice of 1 lime

Salsa Topping

1	avocado, diced
6	scallions (spring onions), thinly sliced
2	red chilies, finely chopped
2	tablespoons fresh cilantro (coriander), chopped
	Freshly squeezed juice of 1 lime

Serves 8–10 • Preparation 30 minutes + 12 hours to soak • Cooking $1^{1}/_2$ hours • Difficulty 1

Soup

1. Soak the beans overnight in a bowl of cold water. Drain.

2. Heat the oil in a soup pot over low heat. Add the onions, carrots, celery, garlic, bouquet garni, and pancetta. Cover and sweat on low heat until tender, 10–15 minutes.

3. Add the beans and enough water to cover by about 3 inches (8 cm). Bring to a boil then cover and simmer on low until the beans are very tender, about 1 hour.

4. Add the tomatoes, cumin, oregano, salt, pepper, sherry, and lime juice and simmer for 10 minutes.

Salsa Topping

1. Combine the avocado, scallions, chilies, and cilantro in a bowl. Drizzle with the lime juice.

2. Ladle the soup into eight to ten soup bowls and top each one with some of the salsa topping. Serve hot.

This oriental soup is packed with flavor and goodness. Serve hot as a complete light meal in itself. Because the beef is cooked right at the end with the heat of the soup, make sure that it is very thinly sliced and that the soup you ladle over it is boiling hot.

ORIENTAL BEEF & NOODLE soup

2	pounds (1 kg) beef bones
3	quarts (3 liters) cold water
2	large onions, chopped
1	(2-inch/5-cm) piece ginger, thinly sliced
5	star anise
2	cinnamon sticks
1	teaspoon black peppercorns
5	whole cloves
1	tablespoon coriander seeds
2	tablespoons Thai fish sauce
2	tablespoons lime juice + wedges, to serve
	Freshly ground sea salt and black pepper
4	ounces (120 g) thick rice noodles
8	ounces (250 g) lean beef fillet steak, very thinly sliced
2	cups (100 g) bean sprouts
3	scallions (spring onions), thinly sliced
2	red chilies, thinly sliced
1/2	cup fresh mint leaves
1/2	cup fresh cilantro (coriander) leaves

Serves 6 • Preparation 15 minutes • Cooking 3$\frac{1}{2}$ hours • Difficulty 2

1. Combine the beef bones, water, onions, ginger, star anise, cinnamon, peppercorns, cloves, and coriander seeds in a large soup pot over high heat. Bring to a boil, then simmer on low for 3 hours, skimming the surface occasionally with a slotted spoon. The liquid should reduce by about half.

2. Remove from the heat and strain through a fine-mesh sieve into a clean pot. Remove and reserve any meat from the bones and discard the remaining solids.

3. Place the soup over high heat and bring to a boil. Add the fish sauce and lime juice and stir to combine. Season with salt and pepper.

4. Meanwhile, place the noodles in a large heatproof bowl and cover with boiling water. Let soak for 5 minutes, or according to the instructions on the package. Drain well.

5. Divide the noodles evenly among six serving bowls. Top with the sliced beef and any reserved meat from the bones. Ladle the boiling soup into the bowls, and top with bean sprouts, scallions, chilies, mint, and cilantro.

6. Serve hot, with the lime wedges.

BEEF & VEGGIE soup

2	tablespoons extra-virgin olive oil
1	pound (500 g) beef cheeks, trimmed of any fat, and cut into small cubes
	Freshly ground sea salt and black pepper
2	carrots, finely chopped
2	stalks celery, finely chopped
2	cloves garlic, finely chopped
1	onion, finely chopped
$1/3$	cup (90 g) tomato paste
$1/2$	cup (120 ml) dry red wine
1	(14-ounce/400-g) can chopped tomatoes, with juice
4	cups (1 liter) beef stock
4	ounces (120 g) risoni pasta (orzo)
2	cups (100 g) baby spinach leaves
	Parmesan flakes, to serve
	Pesto, to serve

Serves 6 • Preparation 30 minutes • Cooking 2½ hours • Difficulty 1

1. Heat the oil in a large soup pot over medium-high heat. Season the beef with salt and pepper. Add to the pot in batches and sauté until browned all over, 4–5 minutes each batch. Set aside.

2. Add the carrots, celery, garlic, and onion to the pot and sauté until the vegetables start to soften, about 5 minutes. Return the beef to the pot, along with the tomato paste, and stir for 1 minute. Add the wine, tomatoes, and beef stock and bring to a boil. Partially cover and simmer on low until the beef is very tender, about 2 hours.

3. Add the risoni and cook until al dente. Stir in the spinach and simmer until just wilted, 2–3 minutes.

4. Ladle the soup into serving bowls and serve hot with Parmesan and pesto.

MEATBALL soup

1 pound (500 g) lean ground (minced) pork
2 cloves garlic, finely chopped
1 small onion, finely chopped
4 tablespoons finely chopped fresh parsley
$1/2$ teaspoon red pepper flakes
1 cup (150 g) fine dry bread crumbs
$1/2$ cup (60 g) freshly grated Parmesan cheese + extra, to serve
Freshly ground sea salt and black pepper
2 tablespoons extra-virgin olive oil
6 cups (1.5 liters) chicken stock
$3^{1}/2$ ounces (100 g) angel-hair pasta, broken into short pieces

Serves 6 • Preparation 20 minutes • Cooking 15 minutes • Difficulty 2

1. Combine the pork, garlic, onion, 2 tablespoons of parsley, the red pepper flakes, bread crumbs, and Parmesan in a bowl. Season with salt and pepper. Mix well, then shape into small meatballs.

2. Heat the oil in a large frying pan over medium-low heat. Fry the meatballs until golden brown, 8–10 minutes. Let drain on paper towels.

3. Add the chicken stock to the pan and bring to a boil. Add the pasta and cook for 1 minute. Add the meatballs and simmer gently over low heat until the pasta is cooked al dente, 2–3 minutes.

4. Ladle the soup into serving bowls and garnish with the remaining 2 tablespoons of parsley and the extra Parmesan. Serve hot.

One medium orange has about 15 grams of carbs, so this salad will not send you over the top on your carbs allowance. The black olives and olive oil add flavor as well as healthy monounsaturated fatty acids.

ORANGE & BLACK OLIVE salad

3	fresh oranges
3	cups (150 g) arugula (rocket)
3	cups (150 g) baby spinach leaves
2	small red onions
1	cup (100 g) black olives, pitted and chopped
$^1/_3$	cup (90 ml) extra-virgin olive oil
3	tablespoons red vinegar
	Freshly ground sea salt and black pepper

Serves 6 • Preparation 15 minutes + 15 minutes to rest • Difficulty 1

1. Peel the oranges, discarding any seeds, and use a sharp knife to remove all the external white pith. Break into wedges. Work over a bowl to catch any juices that drip; add them to the dressing.

2. Combine the oranges, arugula, baby spinach, onions, and olives in a large salad bowl.

3. Whisk the oil, vinegar, salt, and pepper together in a bowl and pour over the salad. Toss well.

4. Set aside for 15 minutes before serving.

If you liked this recipe, you will love these as well.

APPLE SALAD
with yogurt dressing

ROASTED PUMPKIN SALAD with lentils & sesame

FREE-RANGE EGG & FRESH HERB salad

APPLE SALAD with yogurt dressing

Dressing

¹/₂	cup (120 ml) plain yogurt
¹/₂	cup (120 ml) mayonnaise
1	tablespoon mustard
1	tablespoon cider vinegar

Salad

1	head romaine (cos) lettuce, coarsely shredded
1	large red organic apple, cored and cut into small cubes
1	large green organic apple, cored and cut into small cubes
1	small head celery, sliced
¹/₂	cup (60 g) walnuts, coarsely chopped
	Freshly ground sea salt and black pepper

Serves 4 • Preparation 15 minutes • Difficulty 1

Dressing

1. Whisk the yogurt, mayonnaise, mustard, and vinegar in a small bowl.

Salad

1. Arrange the lettuce in a large salad bowl. Add the apples, celery, and walnuts. Drizzle with the dressing and season with salt and pepper.

2. Serve at once.

ROASTED PUMPKIN SALAD
with lentils & sesame

Salad

4	pounds (2 kg) pumpkin or butternut squash, peeled and cut into $^3/_4$-inch (2-cm) cubes
2	tablespoons extra-virgin olive oil
	Freshly ground sea salt and black pepper
1	cup (200 g) Le Puy lentils
2	cups (100 g) arugula (rocket)
1	teaspoon sesame seeds
6	scallions (spring onions), sliced

Dressing

$^1/_4$	cup (60 ml) extra-virgin olive oil
2	tablespoons balsamic vinegar
1	red chili, chopped
1	garlic clove, finely chopped
1	teaspoon honey

Serves 6 • Preparation 15 minutes • Cooking 20–30 minutes • Difficulty 1

Salad

1. Preheat the oven to 400°F (200°C/gas 6). Put the squash on a baking sheet, drizzle with the oil and season with salt and pepper.

2. Roast for 20–30 minutes, until tender. Meanwhile, cook the lentils in salted boiling water until tender, 15–20 minutes. Drain well and let cool a little in the colander.

Dressing

1. Whisk the oil, vinegar, chili, garlic, and honey in a small bowl.

2. Put the arugula in a shallow serving bowl and arrange the lentils and squash on top. Drizzle with the dressing, top with the sesame seeds and scallions, and serve.

This traditional French salad is rich in nutritious ingredients that make it a healthy dish for everyone, diabetic or not. You may be surprised to learn that canned tuna can be just as nutritious as fresh, especially if you choose a good quality white albacore packed in water (not oil). Tuna is a great source of protein, contains no carbohydrates, and is also a source of heart-healthy omega-3 fatty acids.

SALADE niçoise

Salad

10	medium firm tomatoes, each one cut into 8 wedges
	Sea salt flakes
3	cups (150 g) mixed salad greens
1	red bell pepper (capsicum), seeded and cut into thin strips
8	ounces (250 g) canned tuna, drained
3	stalks celery, thinly sliced
3	shallots, finely chopped
12	black olives
6–8	salt-cured anchovy fillets
4	hard-boiled eggs, quartered

Vinaigrette

$^1/_3$	cup (90 ml) extra-virgin olive oil
2	tablespoons white wine vinegar
1	teaspoon Dijon mustard
	Freshly ground sea salt and black pepper

Serves 4–6 • Preparation 15 minutes + 1 hour to drain • Difficulty 1

Salad

1. Place the tomatoes in a colander and sprinkle lightly with salt. Let stand for 1 hour to drain.

2. Arrange the salad greens in four to six salad bowls with the tomatoes around the edges. Put the bell pepper, tuna, celery, and shallots in the center. Arrange the olives and anchovy fillets on top. Garnish with the egg wedges.

Vinaigrette

1. Whisk the oil, vinegar, mustard, salt, and pepper in a small bowl until emulsified.

2. Drizzle over the salad, and serve.

If you liked this recipe, you will love these as well.

ORANGE & BLACK OLIVE salad

FREE-RANGE EGG & FRESH HERB salad

FETA & FAVA BEAN salad

FREE-RANGE EGG & FRESH HERB salad

8	large eggs
$1/4$	cup finely chopped fresh parsley
$1/4$	cup finely chopped fresh dill
$1/4$	cup finely chopped fresh chives
$1/4$	cup finely chopped fresh tarragon
2	stalks celery, finely chopped
1	small red onion, finely chopped
	Freshly ground sea salt and black pepper
1	tablespoon white wine vinegar
2	tablespoons freshly squeezed lemon juice
$1/3$	cup (90 ml) plain yogurt
1	tablespoon mayonnaise
1	clove garlic, finely chopped
1	teaspoon Dijon mustard
2	tablespoons extra-virgin olive oil
4	cups (200 g) baby arugula (rocket)

Serves 4 • Preparation 15 minutes • Cooking 7–8 minutes • Difficulty 1

1. Lower the eggs into boiling water and boil for 7–8 minutes. Place in a bowl of cold water to cool. When cool enough to handle, shell, and chop coarsely.

2. Combine the chopped eggs, parsley, dill, chives, tarragon, celery and onion in a large bowl. Season to taste with salt and pepper.

3. Whisk the vinegar, lemon juice, yogurt, mayonnaise, mustard, and oil in a small bowl. Season with salt and pepper. Toss with the egg mixture.

4. Line four serving plates or bowls with arugula, top with the egg salad, and serve.

COUSCOUS TABBOULEH *salad*

5 tablespoons (75 ml) extra-virgin olive oil

1 cup (150 g) fine or medium grain whole-wheat (wholemeal) couscous

Sea salt flakes

2¾ cups (700 ml) boiling water

½ cup (120 ml) freshly squeezed lemon juice

½ teaspoon ground cumin

1 red bell pepper (capsicum), seeded and diced

1 pound (500 g) cherry tomatoes, halved

1 small cucumber, diced

4 scallions (spring onions), thinly sliced

1 cup (50 g) finely chopped fresh parsley

¼ cup finely chopped fresh mint

Freshly ground black pepper

Small romaine lettuce leaves, for scoops, to serve (optional)

Serves 4 • Preparation 15 minutes + 30 minutes to cool & stand
Cooking 1–2 minutes • Difficulty 1

1. Heat 1 tablespoon of oil in a medium saucepan over medium heat. Add the couscous, stir to coat the grains, then cook for 1–2 minutes. Remove from the heat, add ½ teaspoon of salt and 2 cups (500 ml) of the boiling water. Shake the pan, cover, and let stand for 7 minutes.

2. Fluff the couscous with a fork, then pour in the remaining boiling water, half the lemon juice, and the cumin. Cover and let stand for 5 minutes.

3. Put the couscous in a salad bowl. Let cool for 15 minutes.

4. Add the bell pepper, cherry tomatoes, cucumber, scallions, parsley, and mint, and toss well.

5. Whisk the remaining 4 tablespoons of oil and the remaining lemon juice in a bowl. Season with salt and pepper.

6. Drizzle the dressing over the salad. Serve with the romaine lettuce leaves as scoops, if liked.

GREEK salad

Serves 4 • Preparation 15 minutes • Difficulty 1

Salad

24	cherry tomatoes, halved	20	black olives, preferably kalamata
1	red onion, thinly sliced	1	teaspoon finely chopped unwaxed lemon zest
2	cups (100 g) mixed baby salad greens		

Dressing

¼	cup coarsely chopped fresh parsley	¼ cup (60 ml) extra-virgin olive oil
¼	cup coarsely chopped fresh mint	Freshly squeezed juice of 1 lemon
5	ounces (150 g) feta cheese, crumbled	Salt and freshly ground black pepper

Salad

1. Combine the cherry tomatoes, onion, salad greens, parsley, mint, feta, olives, and lemon zest in a large salad bowl. Toss gently.

Dressing

1. Whisk the oil, lemon juice, salt, and pepper in a small bowl until well mixed.

2. Drizzle the dressing over the salad and serve.

CHICKEN SALAD with mango

Serves 4-6 • Preparation 15 minutes • Difficulty 1

Salad

1	roasted or barbecued chicken	1	long red chili, seeded and thinly sliced
4	cups (200 g) mixed salad greens	½	cup (60 g) toasted walnuts
2	mangoes, peeled, cut into small cubes		

Dressing

2	avocados, peeled, pitted, and cut into small cubes	⅓	cup (90 ml) extra-virgin olive oil
½	cup fresh cilantro (coriander)	2	tablespoons balsamic vinegar
		2	teaspoons Dijon mustard
		1-2	teaspoons honey

Salad

1. Remove the flesh from the chicken. Discard the skin and bones. Shred the chicken flesh.

2. Combine the chicken flesh, salad greens, mangoes, avocados, cilantro, chili, and walnuts in a salad bowl.

Dressing

1. Whisk the oil, vinegar, mustard, and honey in a small bowl. Season with salt and pepper.

2. Drizzle the dressing over the salad, and serve.

FETA & FAVA BEAN salad

Serves 6-8 • Preparation 15 minutes • Cooking 3-4 minutes Difficulty 1

Salad

1	pound (500 g) fresh or frozen fava (broad) beans	4	pita breads, toasted, torn into small pieces
1	cup (150 g) fresh or frozen peas	7	ounces (200 g) feta cheese, crumbled
1	cucumber		

Dressing

2	tablespoons coarsely chopped fresh mint		Finely grated zest and freshly squeezed juice of 1 unwaxed lemon
4	tablespoons coarsely chopped fresh parsley	⅓	cup (90 ml) extra-virgin olive oil
	Fresh chives, snipped	1	teaspoon brown sugar
			Freshly ground sea salt and black pepper

Salad

1. Boil the beans and peas in salted water until just tender, 3-4 minutes. Drain well and set aside.

2. Halve the cucumber lengthwise, scrape out the seeds, then slice. Add to the bean mixture.

Dressing

1. Whisk the dressing ingredients in a small bowl. Pour over the bean mixture. Add the mint, parsley, chives, pita, and feta. Toss gently and serve.

FARRO salad

Serves 8 • Preparation 15 minutes + 1-2 hours to stand Cooking about 40 minutes • Difficulty 1

2	cups (400 g) farro	1	cup (50 g) coarsely chopped fresh basil leaves
24	cherry tomatoes, halved	2	tablespoons capers
8	ounces (250 g) mozzarella cheese, diced		Freshly ground sea salt and black pepper
6	scallions (spring onions), chopped	⅓	cup (90 ml) extra-virgin olive oil
1-2	cloves garlic, minced		

1. Cook the farro in a pot of salted, boiling water for the time indicated on the package. Drain and let cool a little in the colander.

2. Transfer to a bowl. Add the tomatoes, mozzarella, scallions, garlic, basil, capers, salt, pepper, and oil, mix well.

3. Set aside for 1-2 hours before serving.

a gourmet cookbook for diabetics

CHICKEN & CORN salad

2	ears (cobs) fresh corn (sweetcorn), with husks
1/4	cup (60 g) butter, softened
2	tablespoons harissa or chili paste
	Finely grated zest and juice of 1 untreated lemon
2	tablespoons finely chopped fresh parsley
	Freshly ground sea salt and black pepper
2	boneless skinless chicken breasts
4	tablespoons (60 ml) extra-virgin olive oil
	Pinch of cayenne pepper
1	red bell pepper (capsicum), seeded and sliced
1	avocado, pitted and sliced
4	cups (200 g) lamb's lettuce
	Small bunch fresh chives, snipped

Serves 4 • Preparation 30 minutes • Cooking 15–20 minutes • Difficulty 2

1. Peel back the corn husks, leaving them attached at the base. Blend the butter, harissa, lemon zest, and parsley in a bowl. Season with salt and pepper. Smear over the corn, then re-cover with the leaves and tie with kitchen string.

2. Preheat a grill pan (griddle) to hot. Grill the ears of corn in their husks, turning often, until blackened all over and tender, 15–20 minutes. Set aside.

3. Flatten the chicken breasts lightly with a meat tenderizer. Brush with 1 tablespoon of oil and season with salt, pepper, and cayenne. Grill until cooked through, 6–10 minutes.

4. Combine the bell pepper, avocado, and lamb's lettuce in a salad bowl and toss gently.

5. Whisk the remaining 3 tablespoons of oil with the lemon juice, salt, and pepper in a small bowl. Drizzle over the salad and toss gently. Slice the chicken and add to the salad.

6. Remove the husks from the corn and use a sharp knife to strip off the kernels. Add to the salad. Toss well, sprinkle with the chives, and serve warm.

CHICKEN, BEAN & AVOCADO *salad*

2	tablespoons extra-virgin olive oil
1	teaspoon ground cumin
1	teaspoon chili powder
2	boneless skinless chicken breasts
24	cherry tomatoes, halved
1	red onion, thinly sliced
4	small iceberg lettuce hearts, sliced
1/2	cup (25 g) fresh cilantro (coriander)
3	avocados, peeled and thickly sliced
1/2	cup (120 ml) Caesar dressing
1	(14-ounce/400-g) can butter beans, drained and rinsed

Serves 4–6 • Preparation 10 minutes • Cooking 10–15 minutes
Difficulty 1

1. Whisk the oil, cumin, and chili powder in a large bowl. Add the chicken and coat well.

2. Pan-fry the chicken (without extra oil) in a large frying pan for a few minutes each side. Toss the tomatoes in any spiced oil left in the bowl, then add to the pan. Cover and simmer for 5 minutes, until the chicken is cooked and the tomatoes are starting to soften.

3. Toss the onion, lettuce, cilantro, and avocados in the Caesar dressing and pile onto a large platter.

4. Top with the beans and scatter with the tomatoes. Slice the warm chicken and toss gently with the salad. Serve warm.

66

Protein foods are an important part of any healthy meal plan. Red meats, such as steak, do not contain carbohydrates so will not raise your blood sugar levels. However, they can be high in fats so be sure to choose lean cuts such as chuck, rib, rump roast, round, sirloin, cubed, flank, porterhouse, T-bone steak, or tenderloin, and be sure to trim off any visible fat.

STEAK & TOMATO salad

4	sirloin steaks
2	teaspoons paprika
4	tablespoons (60 ml) extra-virgin olive oil
	Freshly ground sea salt and black pepper
1	red onion, thinly sliced
30	cherry tomatoes, halved
	Bunch of fresh cilantro (coriander), coarsely chopped
2	tablespoons balsamic vinegar

Serves 4–6 • Preparation 15 minutes • Cooking 10–15 minutes
Difficulty 1

1. Rub the steaks on both sides with 1 teaspoon of the paprika and 2 tablespoons of the oil. Season with salt and pepper.

2. Preheat a grill pan (griddle), overhead broiler (grill), or barbecue grill on medium heat. Grill or broil the steaks until cooked to your liking, 3–4 minutes on each side for medium-rare, 6–7 minutes for well done.

3. Remove from the heat and let rest for 5 minutes before slicing into strips.

4. Combine the onion, cherry tomatoes, cilantro, remaining paprika, and remaining 2 tablespoons of oil, and vinegar in a bowl. Season with salt and pepper.

5. Toss the salad gently with the sliced steak, and serve warm.

If you liked this recipe, you will love these as well.

CHICKEN SALAD
with mango

CHICKEN & CORN
salad

CHICKEN, BEAN & AVOCADO salad

main dishes

TUNA BURGERS with roasties & salad

Serves 4 • Preparation 30 minutes • Cooking 60–65 minutes • Difficulty 1

Roasties

1¹/₂	pounds (750 g) roasting potatoes, quartered
3	cloves garlic, sliced
³/₄	cup (180 ml) vegetable stock
2	tablespoons extra-virgin olive oil
	Sea salt flakes and freshly ground black pepper

Burgers

4	boneless, skinless tuna steaks, about 1¹/₄ pounds (600 g) in total, cut into chunks
2	tablespoons Thai red curry paste
2	teaspoons finely grated fresh ginger
1	teaspoon soy sauce
1	bunch fresh cilantro (coriander), half chopped, half leaves picked
1	teaspoon extra-virgin olive oil
	Lemon wedges, to serve

Salad

2	carrots
1	small cucumber
2	tablespoons apple cider vinegar
1	teaspoon superfine (caster) sugar

Roasties

1. Preheat the oven to 400°F (200°C/gas 6).

2. Put the potatoes and garlic in a roasting pan. Pour in the stock, then brush the tops of the potatoes with half the oil. Season with salt and pepper. Roast for 50 minutes.

3. Brush the potatoes with the remaining oil and cook 10–15 more minutes, until the stock is absorbed and the potatoes are browned and cooked through.

Burgers

1. Combine the tuna in a food processor with the red curry paste, ginger, soy, and chopped cilantro. Pulse until coarsely minced. Shape into four burgers.

2. Heat the oil in a non-stick frying pan over medium heat. Add the burgers and cook until crisp and cooked through, 4–5 minutes on each side.

Salad

1. Use a potato peeler to peel long thin strips of carrot and cucumber into a bowl. Toss with the cider vinegar and sugar until the sugar has dissolved. Add the remaining cilantro leaves and toss again.

2. Serve the burgers hot with the roasties and salad.

Tofu is made by curdling soymilk so that its proteins become coagulated. It is then pressed into a sliceable cake. Tofu is rich in antioxidants that can reduce cancer risk, lower cholesterol, and improve insulin and blood sugar metabolism.

SPICY TOFU & VEGETABLE stir-fry

12	ounces (350 g) firm tofu, cut into $^1/_2$-inch (2-cm) cubes
1	teaspoon black peppercorns
1	teaspoon salt
$^1/_4$	teaspoon Chinese five-spice powder
1	tablespoon cornstarch (cornflour)
2	tablespoons peanut oil
1	pound (500 g) sprouting broccoli
2	shallots, peeled
2	tablespoons peanut oil
1	teaspoon grated ginger
2	red chilies, sliced thinly
1	tablespoon grated palm sugar or brown sugar
1-2	tablespoons water, if needed
4	ounces (120 g) shiitake mushrooms, halved
1	clove garlic, sliced
2	tablespoons lime juice
$^1/_3$	cup (90 ml) light soy sauce
	Large bunch fresh basil, coarsely chopped
2	tablespoons unsalted roasted peanuts, coarsely chopped
2	scallions (spring onions), sliced
	Limes wedges, to serve

Serves 4 • Preparation 20 minutes + 30 minutes to drain • Cooking 12-15 minutes • Difficulty 2

1. Spread the tofu in a single layer on paper towels. Cover with more towels and let drain for 30 minutes.

2. Heat a frying pan and dry-fry the peppercorns until fragrant, about 1 minute. Transfer to a mortar and add the salt and five-spice powder. Pound to a fine powder using the pestle. Mix in the cornstarch and set aside.

3. Trim the broccoli and cut into stems and florets. Thinly slice the shallots.

4. Coat the tofu cubes in the spice mix, shaking off any excess. Heat the oil in a wok or large frying pan. When really hot, stir-fry the tofu in batches until lightly golden with a thin crust all over. Drain on paper towels.

5. Before you cook the vegetables, remove any sediment from the pan with paper towels.

6. Heat the oil and stir-fry the shallots, ginger, and chilies over medium heat until softened, 5-8 minutes. Add the sugar and stir-fry until dissolved.

7. Turn up the heat and add the broccoli, shaking the pan and adding a splash of water if it dries out. Stir until tender, 2-3 minutes. Add the mushrooms and garlic, and stir-fry for 1 minute. Pour in the lime juice and soy sauce, and stir gently until combined.

8. Add the basil and tofu and cook until warmed through, 2-3 minutes. Sprinkle with the peanuts and scallions. Serve hot with the lime wedges.

PORTOBELLO burgers

¹/₄ cup (60 ml) extra-virgin olive oil

¹/₄ cup (60 ml) balsamic vinegar

3 cloves garlic, finely chopped

Freshly ground sea salt and black pepper

1 red bell pepper (capsicum), seeded and quartered

8 portobello mushrooms, stalks removed

4 hamburger buns or round bread rolls, halved

5 ounces (150 g) fresh goat cheese

1 cup (50 g) fresh baby salad greens

4 tablespoons storebought or homemade chutney

Serves 4 • Preparation 20 minutes + 30 minutes to marinate • Cooking 15–20 minutes • Difficulty 1

1. Whisk the oil, vinegar, garlic, salt, and pepper in a bowl. Add the bell pepper and mushrooms, tossing gently to coat. Marinate at room temperature for 30 minutes.

2. Preheat a grill pan (griddle) to medium-high. Brush with oil.

3. Grill the bell peppers until the skins are blackened, 7–10 minutes. Place in a bowl, cover with plastic wrap (cling film), and let rest for 10 minutes. Peel off the skin.

4. Grill the mushrooms until lightly charred and tender, 3–4 minutes each side. Place the buns cut-side down on the grill and lightly toast.

5. Spread the bottoms of the buns with goat cheese, and top with the salad greens, mushrooms, bell pepper, and chutney. Cover with the tops of the buns, and serve hot.

LENTIL BURGERS with yogurt & lemon dressing

½ cup (120 ml) plain low-fat yogurt

¼ cup (60 ml) freshly squeezed lemon juice

2 tablespoons tahini (sesame paste)

Freshly ground sea salt and black pepper

1 cup (200 g) cold mashed potato

1 (14-ounce/400-g) can brown lentils, rinsed, drained

1 tablespoon mild Indian curry paste

4 scallions (spring onions), thinly sliced

1 free-range egg

½ cup (75 g) fine dry bread crumbs + extra, as required

1 tablespoon extra-virgin olive oil

4 multigrain burger buns, halved

2 medium tomatoes, sliced

Watercress, to serve

Serves 4 • Preparation 15 minutes + 30 minutes to chill • Cooking 8–10 minutes • Difficulty 1

1. Combine the yogurt, lemon juice, and tahini in a small bowl. Season with salt and pepper and chill until ready to serve.

2. Combine the mashed potato, lentils, curry paste, scallions, egg, and bread crumbs in a large bowl. Season with salt and pepper. Use your hands to bring the mixture together.

3. Shape into four even patties, using extra bread crumbs as required to help shape the patties. Chill for 30 minutes.

4. Heat the oil in a large frying pan over medium heat. Cook the patties until golden and warmed through, 3–5 minutes on each side.

5. Preheat an overhead grill and lightly toast the buns.

6. Cover the bottoms of the buns with watercress. Top with the hot patties, tomatoes, and yogurt dressing. Serve hot.

a gourmet cookbook for diabetics

TOFU & VEGGIE burgers

Serves 4–6 • Preparation 10 minutes • Cooking 15 minutes
Difficulty 1

1	carrot, grated	2	free-range eggs, beaten
6	scallions (spring onions), thinly sliced		Freshly ground sea salt and black pepper
2	cloves garlic, minced	2	tablespoons sesame oil
1	tablespoon freshly grated ginger	2	tablespoons extra-virgin olive oil
14	ounces (400 g) firm tofu, drained and crumbled		Sweet chili (chilli) sauce, to serve
			Salad greens, to serve

1. Combine the carrot, scallions, garlic, ginger, tofu, and eggs in a large bowl. Season with salt and pepper, mixing well.

2. Heat both types of oil in a frying pan. Grease a 3-inch (8-cm) metal pastry ring or cookie cutter and place in the pan. When hot, pour in 5 tablespoons of the batter and turn the heat down to medium.

3. Cook until golden, 4–5 minutes, then take off the ring, flip the burger and cook the other side. Do this in batches, keeping the finished burgers warm in a low oven.

4. Serve hot, with the chili sauce and salad greens.

SPICY tofu

Serves 6 • Preparation 10 minutes • Cooking 20 minutes
Difficulty 1

2	tablespoons sesame oil	2	red chilies, minced
2	pounds (1 kg) firm tofu, cut into small cubes	1	tablespoon dry sherry
2	scallions (spring onions), finely chopped	1½	tablespoons soy sauce
		1	cup (250 ml) + 1 tablespoons water
2	cloves garlic, minced	½	teaspoon sea salt flakes
1	teaspoon finely chopped fresh ginger	1½	teaspoons cornstarch (cornflour)

1. Heat the oil in a large wok or frying pan over medium-high heat. Add the tofu, half the scallions, half the garlic, and the ginger and stir-fry for 3 minutes. Add the chilies and stir-fry for 1 minute.

2. Stir in the sherry, soy sauce, 1 cup (250 ml) water, and salt. Bring to a boil and simmer for 3 minutes.

3. Mix the remaining water and cornstarch in a small bowl. Stir into the wok and cook until the mixture thickens, 2–3 minutes. Sprinkle with the remaining scallion and garlic.

4. Transfer to heated plates, and serve hot.

BUTTER BEAN casserole

Serves 6 • Preparation 15 minutes + 12 hours to soak
Cooking 2¼ hours • Difficulty 1

2	cups (350 g) dried butter beans		tomatoes, peeled and coarsely chopped
3	tablespoons extra-virgin olive oil	1	teaspoon sugar
1	red onion, minced	1	teaspoon dried oregano
2	cloves garlic, minced	2	tablespoons coarsely chopped fresh parsley
2	tablespoons tomato paste (concentrate)		Freshly ground sea salt and black pepper
1½	pounds (750 g)		

1. Soak the beans overnight in cold water. Drain and rinse. Place in a pan of cold water. Bring to a boil, then simmer until tender, about 1 hour. Drain.

2. Preheat the oven to 350°F (180°C/gas 4).

3. Heat the oil in a Dutch oven over medium heat. Add the onion and garlic and sauté until softened, 3–4 minutes. Add the tomato paste and cook for 1 minute. Add the tomatoes, sugar, oregano, and parsley. Season with salt and pepper and simmer for 5 minutes. Stir in the beans.

4. Bake in the oven for 1 hour, uncovered and without stirring, until the beans are tender. Serve hot.

WHEAT BERRIES with walnuts

Serves 6 • Preparation 30 minutes + 12 hours to soak
Cooking 1–2 hours • Difficulty 1

2	cups (350 g) wheat berries		chopped fresh mint + extra, to garnish
4	zucchini (courgettes), thinly sliced lengthwise	6	tablespoons (90 ml) extra-virgin olive oil
	Freshly ground sea salt and black pepper	1	tablespoon freshly squeezed lemon juice
2	tablespoons finely chopped fresh parsley	20	walnuts, chopped
1	tablespoon finely	3½	ounces (100 g) Parmesan, in flakes

1. Soak the wheat in cold water for 12 hours. Drain well. Transfer to a large saucepan. Pour in enough hot water to cover the wheat by about 2 inches (5 cm). Bring to a boil, then simmer until tender, 1–2 hours.

2. Meanwhile, preheat a grill pan (griddle) and grill the zucchini until tender and marked with brown lines, 2–3 minutes each side. Transfer to a bowl. Season with salt and pepper, and drizzle with 2 tablespoons of the oil. Sprinkle with the parsley and mint.

3. Drain the wheat and set aside to cool. Place the zucchini on a large serving dish and spoon the wheat over the top. Drizzle with the remaining oil and the lemon juice.

4. Add the walnuts, cheese and extra mint, and serve.

Check your stocks and make this bean feast with any beans you may have—borlotti, cannellini, haricot, butter, black-eyed, red kidney, pinto, or garbanzo beans (chickpeas). If time is short, use three 14-ounce (400-g) cans of beans, well drained and rinsed. If cooking for a crowd, double the quantities and prepare a day in advance. Chill the casserole in the refrigerator and reheat; the flavors will be even better.

THREE BEAN CHILI casserole

1	cup (175 g) cannellini beans
1	cup (175 g) red kidney beans
1	cup (175 g) black beans
1	large onion, unpeeled
8	sage leaves
4	tablespoons (60 ml) extra-virgin olive oil
2	medium red onions, chopped
1	large white onion, chopped
2	green chilies, finely chopped
3	cloves garlic, finely chopped
1	tablespoon ground cumin
1	tablespoon ground coriander
2	red bell peppers (capsicums), cut into $1/2$-inch (1-cm) dice
2	small potatoes, peeled and cut into $1/2$-inch (1-cm) dice
2	tablespoons tomato paste
1	(14-ounce/400-g) can tomatoes, with juice
$1/2$	cup (120 ml) dry red wine
1	teaspoon dried oregano
	Small bunch fresh parsley, finely chopped
	Large bunch fresh cilantro (coriander), finely chopped + extra, to garnish
1	cup (250 ml) water
	Freshly ground sea salt and black pepper
	Chili (chilli) paste, to taste
1	tablespoon tahini paste
1	cup (250 ml) low-fat, Greek-style plain yogurt
	Finely grated zest and juice of $1/2$ unwaxed lemon

Serves 8-10 • Preparation 15 minutes + 12 hours to soak • Cooking $1^3/_4$-$2^1/_4$ hours • Difficulty 2

1. Soak all the beans overnight in plenty of cold water. Drain and rinse, then place in a pan with the unpeeled onion, sage, and 1 tablespoon of oil and plenty of cold water. Bring to a boil, then simmer until tender but not falling apart, about 1–$1^1/_2$ hours. Leave to cool completely in the cooking liquid, then drain.

2. Heat the remaining 3 tablespoons of oil in a large casserole or heavy-bottomed saucepan over medium-low heat, and add the chopped red and white onions. Sauté until very soft and turning golden, about 10 minutes.

3. Add the chilies, garlic, cumin, and coriander, and stir for 1 minute. Add the bell peppers and potatoes, and stir to coat. Add the tomato paste, tomatoes, and all the beans. Stir in the wine, oregano, parsley, and half the cilantro. Pour in most of the water, mixing well. Season with salt and pepper.

4. Bring to a boil, cover, and simmer over very low heat for about 30 minutes, until the vegetables are tender and the sauce is thick. Add the remaining water if needed. Taste for seasoning and heat. Add a little more salt and some chili paste, if you like it very hot.

5. Stir the tahini, yogurt, lemon juice and zest, and remaining garlic in a small bowl with a fork.

6. Sprinkle the extra cilantro over the chili casserole and serve hot with the yogurt mixture on the side.

SWEET & SOUR tuna steaks

2 tablespoons extra-virgin olive oil + extra, for drizzling

2 medium red onions, thickly sliced

¹/₄ cup (45 g) raisins

¹/₄ cup (60 ml) pomegranate molasses

2 tablespoons honey

1 tablespoon red wine vinegar

4 (7-ounce/200-g) tuna steaks

Coarse sea salt and freshly ground black pepper

2 tablespoons pine nuts, lightly toasted

2 tablespoons coarsely chopped fresh parsley

Steamed green beans, to serve (optional)

Serves 4 • Preparation 15 minutes • Cooking 10–12 minutes • Difficulty 1

1. Prepare a hot fire in an outdoor grill or preheat an indoor grill to high heat. If your grill does not have a solid cook surface, place a grill plate, grill mat, or griddle on the grill to preheat.

2. Heat the oil in a medium saucepan over low-medium heat. Add the onion and raisins and sauté until the onions are softened, 3–4 minutes. Add the pomegranate molasses, honey, and red wine vinegar and simmer until syrupy, about 2 minutes. Keep warm.

3. Drizzle the tuna with oil and season with salt and pepper. Grill until golden brown but still pink in the center, about 2 minutes on each side.

4. Serve the tuna steaks hot, topped with the sweet and sour onions and sprinkled with the pine nuts and parsley.

HOT & SPICY fish cutlets

2   red bell peppers (capsicums), seeded and coarsely chopped

3   fresh long red chilies, seeded and coarsely chopped

3   cloves garlic, coarsely chopped

2   tablespoons white wine vinegar

2   tablespoons extra-virgin olive oil

1   tablespoon ground sweet paprika

1   teaspoon sea salt flakes

1/2 teaspoon freshly ground black pepper

4   (7-ounce/200-g) firm white fish cutlets, such as snapper, blue eye trevalla, monkfish

Serves 4 • Preparation 20 minutes + 1 hour to marinate • Cooking 10 minutes • Difficulty 1

1. Combine the bell peppers, chilies, and garlic in a food processor. Pulse until finely chopped. Add the vinegar, oil, paprika, salt, and pepper and blend to make a coarse paste.

2. Place the fish cutlets in a non-reactive dish. Smear with the paste, cover with plastic wrap (cling film), and refrigerate for 1 hour.

3. Prepare a medium-hot fire in an outdoor grill or preheat an indoor grill to medium-high heat. If your grill does not have a solid cook surface, place a grill plate, grill mat, or griddle on the grill to preheat. Grease with oil.

4. Cut two sheets of parchment paper and place on the hot grill plate. Arrange the marinated fish cutlets on top. Grill until just cooked through, about 5 minutes on each side. Serve hot.

THAI FISH with broccoli

Serves 4 • Preparation 20 minutes • Cooking 10–15 minutes
Difficulty 2

	Freshly squeezed juice of 4 limes	1	tablespoon finely grated fresh ginger
2	tablespoons Thai fish sauce	¼	cup (60 ml) peanut oil
1	teaspoon sugar	4	firm white fish fillets, about 5 ounces/150 g each
2	small red chilies, sliced		
2	long green chilies, finely chopped	½	teaspoon light soy sauce
2	stalks lemongrass, shredded	1	teaspoon rice wine
		14	ounces (400 g) broccoli, in small florets

1. Combine the lime juice, fish sauce, sugar, chilies, lemongrass, and ginger in a small bowl and set aside.

2. Heat the oil in a large frying pan over medium heat until sizzling. Pour in the spice mixture. Add the fish and cook without moving until golden underneath, 2–3 minutes. Turn and cook until golden, 1–2 minutes.

3. Transfer to serving plates, drizzle with the soy sauce and rice wine, and set aside in a warm oven.

4. Increase the heat to medium-high and add the broccoli and 1 tablespoon of water. Stir-fry for 3–4 minutes. Serve hot with the fish and juices.

MARENGO chicken

Serves 4–6 • Preparation 15 minutes • Cooking 1 hour
Difficulty 1

1	chicken, weighing about 4 pounds (2 kg) cut into 6–8 pieces	½	cup (120 ml) dry white wine
¼	cup (60 ml) extra-virgin olive oil	1	tablespoon all-purpose (plain) flour
	Freshly ground black pepper	1	cup (250 ml) beef stock
	Dash of nutmeg + extra, to dust		Freshly squeezed juice of ½ lemon

1. Place the chicken in a heavy-bottomed pan with the butter and sauté over medium-high heat until lightly browned, about 5 minutes. Season with salt, pepper, and nutmeg.

2. Discard any liquid in the pan. Add the wine and stir in the flour. Simmer over low heat until the chicken is tender, about 50 minutes. Add the stock as required during cooking to keep the chicken moist.

3. Arrange the chicken on a serving dish and drizzle with the lemon juice. Serve hot, dusted with nutmeg.

BABY OCTOPUS salad

Serves 4 • Preparation 20 minutes + 4–12 hours to marinate
Cooking 2–3 minutes • Difficulty 1

12	ounces (350 g) fresh baby octopus, cleaned	2	cups (100 g) salad greens
⅓	cup (90 ml) Thai sweet chili sauce	1	cup (50 g) bean sprouts
2	tablespoons freshly squeezed lime juice	1	cucumber, thinly sliced
		8	ounces (250 g) cherry tomatoes, halved
1	tablespoon Thai fish sauce	½	cup fresh cilantro (coriander) leaves
1	tablespoon sesame oil		Lime wedges, to serve

1. Place the octopus in a glass or ceramic bowl. Whisk the chili sauce, lime juice, fish sauce, and sesame oil in a bowl. Pour over the octopus, cover, and chill for 4 hours or overnight. Drain, reserving the marinade.

2. Divide the salad greens evenly among four serving plates. Top with the bean sprouts, cucumber, and tomatoes.

3. Preheat a grill pan to very hot. Add the octopus all at once and toss until cooked through, 2–3 minutes. Set aside. Arrange on top of the salad.

4. Place the marinade in a small saucepan and bring to a boil. Drizzle over the salads and garnish with the cilantro and lime wedges. Serve warm.

GRILLED PEPPERED sirloin

Serves 6 • Preparation 15 minutes • Cooking 5–8 minutes
Difficulty 1

1½	pounds (750 g) sirloin or tenderloin steak, boned		black pepper corns
		4	tablespoons (60 ml) extra-virgin olive oil
	Freshly ground sea salt and black pepper	2–3	cups (100–150 g) baby arugula (rocket) leaves
2–3	tablespoons whole		

1. Put the steak on a work surface and season generously with salt.

2. Put the whole black peppercorns on a work surface and cover with foil. Use a meat tenderizer to smash the pepper, so that the corns are cracked. Sprinkle over the meat, working it into the surface with your fingertips.

3. Preheat a grill pan or barbecue on high. Drizzle with 1 tablespoon of oil. Cook the steak on the grill until browned on the outside and cooked to your liking within, 5–8 minutes depending on how thick the steak is and how well done you like it.

4. Put the arugula in a bowl, season with salt and pepper, and drizzle with the remaining 3 tablespoons of oil. Toss well to coat.

5. Slice the steak and serve hot with the arugula.

TURKEY & MANGO curry

Curry Paste

4	chilies, seeded and chopped
2	leeks, white part only, chopped
6	cloves garlic, chopped
1	coriander root, chopped
	Zest of 2 limes, green part only
2	teaspoons cumin seeds
2	teaspoons Thai fish sauce

Curry

2	tablespoons peanut oil
$1^1/_2$	pounds (750 g) turkey breast, cut in bite-size chunks
$^1/_2$	cup (120 ml) low-fat coconut milk
$^1/_2$	cup (120 ml) vegetable stock
2	teaspoons sugar
3	teaspoons soy sauce
2	teaspoons Worcestershire sauce
2	small mangos, pitted and chopped
	Fresh cilantro (coriander) leaves, to garnish

Curry Paste

1. Blend the chilies, leeks, garlic, coriander root, lime zest, cumin, and fish sauce in a mortar and pestle or small food processor until smooth.

Curry

1. Heat the oil in a deep frying-pan over medium-high heat and add $1^1/_2$ tablespoons of the curry paste. Cook for 2 minutes.

2. Add the turkey, coconut milk, vegetable stock, sugar, soy sauce, and Worcestershire sauce. Stir well and bring to a boil. Reduce the heat and simmer until the turkey is tender, about 45 minutes.

3. Add the mango and cook for 2 more minutes. Serve hot with the rice, garnished with cilantro.

TURKEY BREAST IN PANCETTA with veggies

3   pounds (1.5 kg) turkey breast

2–3   tablespoons mixed chopped fresh sage, rosemary, and garlic

      Freshly ground sea salt and black pepper

4   ounces (120 g) very thinly sliced pancetta or prosciutto

2   tablespoons extra-virgin olive oil

1   pound (500 g) white baby onions, peeled

2–3   carrots, sliced

1   pound (500 g) sweet potatoes, cut into small cubes

1   cup (250 ml) dry white wine

2   cups (500 ml) vegetable stock

Serves 6–8 • Preparation 30 minutes • Cooking 1 hour • Difficulty 2

1. Use a sharp knife to open the turkey breast out into a rectangular shape. Pound lightly with a meat tenderizer, taking care not to tear the meat. Sprinkle with the herb mixture, salt, and pepper.

2. Roll the meat up and sprinkle with a little more salt and pepper. Wrap the rolled turkey in the pancetta so that it is completely covered. Tie carefully with kitchen string.

3. Transfer to a heavy-bottomed saucepan and add the oil. Sauté over high heat, turning all the time, until the meat is evenly browned. After about 10 minutes, add the onions, carrots, and potatoes and simmer for 5 minutes.

4. Pour in the wine, cover, and simmer on low until the meat and vegetables are tender, about 50 minutes. Add stock as required to keep the meat moist—the bottom of the pan should always be covered with liquid.

5. Untie the turkey, slice, and arrange on a serving dish with the vegetables. Serve hot with the cooking juices spooned over the top.

This elegant dish comes from Rome. It has less than 250 calories and only about 13 grams of carbs, so is perfectly suited to a healthy diabetes diet. It goes beautifully with steamed vegetables, such as broccoli or carrots.

ROMAN-STYLE VEAL ESCALOPES
with broccoli

8	veal escalopes, about 1 pound (500 g) total weight
$1/3$	cup (50 g) all-purpose (plain) flour
4	large thin slices top-quality prosciutto
8	fresh sage leaves
2	tablespoons butter
2	tablespoons extra-virgin olive oil
	Freshly ground sea salt and black pepper
$1/2$	cup (120 ml) dry white wine
1	pound (500 g) broccoli

Serves 4 • Preparation 15 minutes • Cooking 10–15 minutes • Difficulty 1

1. Trim off any little pieces of fat from the escalopes. Place the on a clean work surface and gently roll with a rolling pin to stretch and flatten to an even thickness. Dredge in the flour, shaking to eliminate any excess.

2. Place half a slice of prosciutto on each scaloppine and top with a sage leaf. Use a toothpick to fix the prosciutto and sage to the veal.

3. Melt the butter and oil in a large sauté pan over medium-high heat. Add the scaloppine with the prosciutto facing downward. Brown on both sides, about 1 minute each side. Season with salt and pepper.

4. Pour in the wine and simmer for 5–6 minutes more.

5. Meanwhile, steam the broccoli until tender, 7–8 minutes.

6. Serve the escalopes hot, with the broccoli on the side.

If you liked this recipe, you will love these as well.

SWEET & SOUR
tuna steaks

GRILLED PEPPERED
sirloin

TURKEY BREAST IN PANCETTA with veggies

CHICKEN TAJINE with prunes

1	chicken, weighing about 4 pounds (2 kg), cut into 6-8 pieces
3	large onions, sliced
$1/3$	cup (90 g) butter
1	stick cinnamon
$1/4$	teaspoon saffron threads
	Freshly ground sea salt and black pepper
$1^1/_2$	cups (375 ml) water
1	cup (200 g) pitted prunes
2	tablespoons honey
2	tablespoons freshly squeezed lemon juice
1	tablespoon sesame seeds
$3/4$	cup (120 g) almonds

Serves 4-6 • Preparation 15 minutes • Cooking 70-80 minutes
Difficulty 1

1. Combine the chicken, onions, butter, cinnamon, saffron, salt, pepper, and water in a large saucepan. Cover and simmer over low heat for 40-45 minutes, stirring occasionally. Remove the chicken and keep warm.

2. Add the prunes to the liquid and simmer until softened, 10-15 minutes. Add the honey and lemon juice and simmer over low heat until reduced by half, about 10 minutes.

3. Return the chicken to the pan and simmer for 10 minutes. Sprinkle with the sesame seeds and almonds. Serve hot.

MEAT LOAF with tomato sauce

1½ pounds (750 g) lean ground (minced) beef

1 large egg

4 ounces (120 g) highly flavored pork sausage, crumbled

Dash of nutmeg (optional)

1 cup (60 g) fresh bread crumbs bread, soaked in 2 tablespoons milk and squeezed dry

1 clove garlic, finely chopped

2 tablespoons finely chopped fresh parsley + extra, to garnish

Freshly ground sea salt and black pepper

¼ cup (30 g) all-purpose (plain) flour

4 tablespoons (60 ml) extra-virgin olive oil

1 small onion, finely chopped

1 small carrot, finely chopped

1 small stalk celery, finely chopped

2 cups (500 g) peeled and chopped fresh or canned tomatoes

1 cup (250 ml) vegetable stock

Serves 6 • Preparation 30 minutes • Cooking 1½ hours • Difficulty 2

1. Mix the beef with the egg, sausage, nutmeg, bread, garlic, and parsley in a bowl. Season with salt and pepper. Shape the mixture into a meat loaf. Put the flour in a large dish and carefully roll the meat loaf in it.

2. Heat 2 tablespoons of oil in a large heavy-bottomed pan over medium heat and carefully brown the meat loaf all over, about 10 minutes. Drain the meat loaf of the cooking oil and set aside.

3. Heat the remaining 2 tablespoons of oil in a sauté pan. Add the onion, carrot, and celery and sauté for 4–5 minutes. Add the tomatoes and simmer for 5 minutes. Place the meat loaf in the pan. Season with salt and pepper. Partially cover the pan and simmer over low heat for about 1 hour. Stir frequently, so that the meat loaf does not stick. If the sauce becomes too dense, add some of the stock.

4. Set aside to cool. Slice the tepid meatloaf and arrange on a serving dish. Heat the sauce just before serving and pour over the slices. Serve hot, garnished with parsley.

side dishes

GRILLED EGGPLANT with exotic spices

2 medium eggplant (aubergines)

Coarse sea salt

2 tablespoons malt vinegar

1 fresh long red chili, seeded and finely chopped

2 teaspoons peeled and finely grated fresh ginger

2 teaspoons superfine (caster) sugar

1 clove garlic, finely chopped

1 teaspoon ground cumin

$1/2$ teaspoon brown mustard seeds, lightly toasted

$1/4$ teaspoon ground turmeric

$1/4$ cup (60 ml) extra-virgin olive oil + extra, for drizzling

2 vine-ripened tomatoes, coarsely chopped

Small handful fresh cilantro (coriander) + extra, coarsely chopped, to garnish

$1/3$ cup (90 ml) fat-free or low-fat plain Greek-style yogurt

Serves 4 • Preparation 20 minutes + 30 minutes to drain • Cooking 6–8 minutes • Difficulty 1

1. Trim the eggplant and cut lengthwise into $2/3$-inch (1.5-cm) thick slices. Arrange on a rack and sprinkle with the coarse sea salt. Set aside for 30 minutes to drain. Rinse carefully under cold running water and pat dry with paper towels.

2. Combine the malt vinegar, chili, ginger, sugar, garlic, cumin, mustard seeds, and turmeric in a bowl. Gradually pour in the oil, whisking with a fork to combine. Add the tomatoes and cilantro and stir to combine.

3. Preheat a grill pan (griddle) to medium heat or prepare a medium fire in an outdoor grill.

4. Drizzle the eggplant with oil and grill until tender and marked with brown lines, 3–4 minutes on each side. Cut into bite-size pieces and place in a medium bowl. Add the spiced tomato mixture and stir to combine.

5. Drizzle with the yogurt, sprinkle with cilantro, and serve.

If you liked this recipe, you will love these as well.

GRILLED ZUCCHINI & FAVA BEANS with spinach

GRILLED CAULIFLOWER with pine nuts

GRILLED baby onions

Quinoa is a very healthy choice for everyone, including diabetics. It is rich in dietary fiber and has a low glycemic index so you will feel full for longer and your blood sugar levels will not spike after eating it. Furthermore, it is an excellent lean plant protein and, unlike other grains, has all the amino acids needed to make a complete protein.

In this recipe we have used quinoa instead of rice in a reinterpretation of a classic Indian dish. It is quite a hearty dish and could also be served in its own.

QUINOA biryani

1	tablespoon butter
1	tablespoon sunflower oil
1	large onion, diced
3	cloves garlic, crushed
1	green bell pepper, (capsicum) seeded and chopped
2	zucchini (courgettes), cut in half lengthwise and sliced
1	teaspoon ground cumin
4	cardamom pods, seeds scooped out and pounded
1	teaspoon mustard seeds
2	teaspoons ground coriander
1/2	teaspoon ground ginger
	Pinch of saffron threads
1	cup (200 g) quinoa
1²/₃	cups (400 ml) water
2	tablespoons finely chopped fresh parsley
2	tablespoons finely chopped fresh cilantro (coriander) + extra sprigs, to garnish
1	tablespoon finely chopped fresh basil
	Freshly ground sea salt and black pepper
2	tablespoons toasted pine nuts
2	tablespoons golden raisins (sultanas)

Serves 4 • Preparation 15 minutes • Cooking 35 minutes • Difficulty 2

1. Heat the butter and oil in a large frying pan over medium heat. Add the onion and garlic and sauté until softened, 3–4 minutes.

2. Add the bell pepper, zucchini, cumin, cardamom, mustard seeds, coriander, ginger, and saffron, and cook for 3 more minutes, stirring frequently.

3. Rinse the quinoa well under cold running water. Add the quinoa and water to the vegetables in the pan and bring to a boil. Cover tightly with a lid and simmer over very low heat for 15 minutes.

4. Stir in the parsley, cilantro, and basil and simmer until the quinoa is tender and the water has been absorbed, about 5 minutes. Fluff the biryani up with a fork and season with salt and pepper.

5. Garnish with the pine nuts, sultanas, and cilantro, and serve.

If you liked this recipe, you will love these as well.

WHEAT BERRIES
with walnuts

**SWEET POTATO
& VEGGIE** stew

LENTIL & PUMPKIN
tajine

GRILLED ZUCCHINI & FAVA BEANS with spinach

2 cups (300 g) fresh or frozen fava (broad) beans

2 medium zucchini (courgettes), trimmed

1/4 cup (60 ml) extra-virgin olive oil + extra, for drizzling

2 tablespoon freshly squeezed lemon juice

1 teaspoon Dijon mustard

1 teaspoon coriander seeds, toasted and crushed

Freshly ground sea salt and black pepper

2 cups (100 g) baby spinach leaves

1 large handful of fresh mint leaves

1 preserved lemon, quartered, pulp discarded, and skin thinly sliced into strips

Serves 4 • Preparation 20 minutes • Cooking 4–5 minutes • Difficulty 1

1. Bring a large pan of water to a boil and blanch the beans until just tender, 1–2 minutes. Drain and refresh in iced water. Drain again. Peel away the tough outer skins. Place the beans in a bowl and set aside.

2. Slice the zucchini lengthwise 1/4-inch (5-mm) thick.

3. Preheat an indoor grill to medium-high heat or prepare a medium-hot fire in an outdoor grill. If your grill does not have a solid cook surface, place a grill plate, grill mat, or griddle on the grill to preheat.

4. Drizzle the zucchini with oil and grill until tender and lightly charred, about 1 minute each side. Leave to cool slightly.

5. Combine the lemon juice, mustard, and coriander seeds in a small bowl. Gradually add the oil, whisking with a fork, until combined. Season with salt and pepper.

6. Add the zucchini, spinach, mint, and preserved lemon to the beans. Pour the dressing over the top and toss to combine. Serve warm.

GRILLED CAULIFLOWER with pine nuts

Cauliflower

1	small head cauliflower
	Extra-virgin olive oil, for drizzling
$1/2$	small red onion, thinly sliced
$1/4$	cup (45 g) pine nuts, lightly toasted
2	tablespoons dried currants
1	tablespoon finely chopped fresh parsley

Dressing

2	tablespoons extra-virgin olive oil
	Freshly squeezed juice of 1 lemon
1	teaspoon ground sumac
$1/2$	teaspoon ground cumin
$1/4$	teaspoon cayenne pepper
	Coarse sea salt and freshly ground black pepper

Serves 4 • Preparation 15 minutes • Cooking 4-6 minutes • Difficulty 1

Cauliflower

1. Preheat an indoor grill to medium-high heat or prepare a medium-hot fire in an outdoor grill. If your grill does not have a solid cook surface, place a grill plate, grill mat, or griddle on the grill to preheat.

2. Remove and discard the leaves from the cauliflower and cut into $1/2$-inch (1-cm) thick slices.

Dressing

1. Combine the oil, lemon juice, sumac, cumin, and cayenne pepper in a small bowl. Season with salt and pepper.

2. Drizzle the cauliflower with oil and grill until lightly charred, 2-3 minutes on each side.

3. Arrange the cauliflower on a plate, sprinkle with the onion, pine nuts, currants, and parsley. Drizzle with the dressing, and serve hot.

SPICY GRILLED zucchini

Serves 4 • Preparation 10 minutes + 1 hour to marinate
Cooking 10 minutes • Difficulty 1

1/4	cup (60 ml) extra-virgin olive oil	1	teaspoon red pepper flakes, or to taste
3	cloves garlic, finely chopped		Sea salt flakes
1	small bunch fresh basil, torn	6	zucchini (courgettes), thinly sliced lengthwise

1. Preheat a grill pan (griddle) over medium heat or prepare a medium-hot fire in a gas or charcoal grill.

2. Mix the oil, garlic, basil, red pepper flakes, and salt in a shallow dish. Add the zucchini and let marinate for 1 hour.

3. Drain the marinade from the zucchini slices. Arrange the zucchini in small batches on the grill. Cook until tender, 3–4 minutes, brushing with the marinade during cooking.

4. Transfer to a serving plate and serve hot or at room temperature.

GRILLED BABY onions

Serves 4–6 • Preparation 10 minutes • Cooking 20 minutes
Difficulty 1

20	small white onions, peeled		Freshly ground sea salt and black pepper
8	bay leaves, cut in half		
1/4	cup (60 ml) extra-virgin olive oil		

1. Preheat a grill pan (griddle) over medium heat or prepare a medium-hot fire in a gas or charcoal grill.

2. Blanch the onions in a pot of salted boiling water for 5 minutes. Drain and dry well.

3. If the onions are large, cut them in half. Thread onto four skewers, alternating with a half bay leaf. Skewer the onions horizontally so that they will lie flat on the grill pan during cooking.

4. Brush generously with oil, and season to taste. Cook on the grill, turning often, until tender and golden brown, about 15 minutes.

5. Season and drizzle with more oil to taste. Serve hot or at room temperature.

SWEET & SOUR bell peppers

Serves 4 • Preparation 15 minutes • Cooking 20 minutes
Difficulty 1

1/4	cup (60 ml) extra-virgin olive oil		Sea salt flakes
1	large onion, finely chopped	2/3	cup (60 g) green olives, pitted and chopped
2	large red bell peppers (capsicums), thinly sliced	2	tablespoons salt-cured capers, rinsed
2	large yellow bell peppers (capsicums), thinly sliced	1/3	cup (90 ml) white wine vinegar
1	(14-ounce/400-g) can tomatoes, with juice	1	tablespoon sugar
		6	tablespoons fine dry bread crumbs
			Fresh basil leaves, to garnish

1. Heat the oil in a large frying pan over medium heat. Add the onion, red and yellow bell peppers, and tomatoes. Season with salt. Sauté until the peppers are almost tender, about 10 minutes. Stir in the olives and capers and simmer for 5 more minutes.

2. Meanwhile, mix the vinegar and sugar in a cup until the sugar has dissolved. Add the mixture to the pan and let it evaporate over high heat for 2 minutes.

3. Add the bread crumbs, mix well and serve hot garnished with the basil.

MUSHROOMS with potatoes

Serves 6 • Preparation 15 minutes • Cooking 20 minutes
Difficulty 1

4	tablespoons (60 ml) extra-virgin olive oil	2	cloves garlic, minced
3	tablespoons finely chopped fresh parsley	1	pound (500 g) wild mushrooms, sliced
2	tablespoons finely chopped fresh marjoram	12	ounces (350 g) button mushrooms, sliced
1	pound (500 g) potatoes, peeled and diced		Freshly ground sea salt and black pepper

1. Heat 3 tablespoons of oil in a frying pan over medium heat. Add 1 tablespoon of parsley and 1 tablespoon of marjoram and sauté for 1 minute. Add the potatoes and 1 clove of garlic. Sauté for 5 minutes.

2. Heat the remaining oil in a large frying pan over medium heat. Add 1 tablespoon of parsley and the remaining marjoram and sauté for 1 minute. Add the wild mushrooms and the remaining garlic and sauté for 2 minutes. Add the button mushrooms and sauté until all the mushrooms tender, 5–7 minutes.

3. Add the mushrooms to the pan with the potatoes and stir over medium heat for 2 minutes. Season with salt and pepper. Sprinkle with the remaining 1 tablespoon parsley. Serve hot.

This tasty stew can be served with meat or fish or as part of a vegetarian spread. It is quite hearty and could also be served alone.

SWEET POTATO & VEGGIE stew

1	tablespoon cumin seeds
1	tablespoon coriander seeds
$^1/_2$	teaspoon mustard seeds
1	dried chili, crumbled
3	cloves
$^1/_2$	teaspoon fenugreek seeds
1	teaspoon turmeric
1	tablespoon vegetable oil
$^1/_2$	tablespoon butter
1	large onion, chopped
2	cloves garlic, sliced
2	teaspoons grated ginger
1	red chili (chilli), chopped
4	large tomatoes, peeled and finely chopped
2	tablespoons lime juice
$1^2/_3$	cups (400 ml) vegetable stock or water
3	potatoes, peeled and cubed
1	small red bell pepper (capsicum), diced
3	medium sweet potatoes, peeled and diced
1	cauliflower, cut into small florets
2	tablespoons chopped fresh mint
	Sea salt flakes
$^3/_4$	cup (180 ml) fat-free or low-fat Greek-style plain yogurt, to serve
2	tablespoons chopped cilantro (coriander)
2	tablespoons cashew nuts, to serve

Serves 4-6 • Preparation 15 minutes • Cooking 35-40 minutes Difficulty 1

1. Dry-fry the cumin, coriander, and mustard seeds, and dried chili in a small frying pan over medium heat, until fragrant and starting to pop, 1–2 minutes. Add the cloves and fenugreek, and grind to a powder in a mill or with a pestle and mortar. Mix in the turmeric.

2. Heat the oil and butter in a large saucepan over medium heat and sauté the onion until softened, 3–4 minutes. Stir in the garlic, ginger, fresh chili, and spice mixture, and cook for 2 minutes.

3. Add the tomatoes, lime juice, and stock, and bring to a boil. Turn down the heat, cover, and simmer for 5 minutes. Add the potatoes and bell pepper, cover, and simmer for 10 minutes. Stir in the sweet potatoes and continue cooking for 10 minutes, until all the potatoes are tender. Make sure they are immersed in the sauce and add a little water if necessary.

4. About 5 minutes before the stew is ready, add the cauliflower and mint. Cook on high heat, uncovered, for a few minutes, until the cauliflower is tender and the sauce has thickened. Season with salt.

5. Serve hot with the yogurt, a sprinkling of cilantro, and the cashews.

LENTIL & PUMPKIN tajine

2	cups (200 g) Le Puy lentils
8	cups (2 liters) water
2	medium tomatoes
3	tablespoons extra-virgin olive oil
1	large onion, diced
4	garlic cloves, finely chopped
1¹/₂	teaspoons sweet paprika
1	teaspoon turmeric
1	teaspoon ground cumin
¹/₂	teaspoon ground cayenne pepper
1	tablespoon tomato paste
¹/₂	teaspoon sugar
1¹/₂	pounds (750 g) winter squash or pumpkin, peeled and cubed
3	tablespoons finely chopped fresh parsley
4	tablespoons chopped fresh cilantro (coriander)
	Freshly ground sea salt and black pepper

Serves 8 • Preparation 30 minutes • Cooking 30–40 minutes • Difficulty 1

1. Put the lentils and water in a medium saucepan over high heat and bring to a boil. Decrease the heat to low, cover, and cook until just tender, 20–30 minutes.

2. Cut the tomatoes in half crosswise and squeeze out the seeds. Coarsely grate the flesh into a small bowl and discard the skins.

3. Heat the oil in a large saucepan over medium heat. Add the onion and garlic and cook until softened, 3–4 minutes. Add the paprika, turmeric, cumin, and cayenne and cook until fragrant, 30 seconds.

4. Add the tomato, tomato paste, and sugar and stir to combine. Add the squash and lentils with their cooking liquid and bring to a boil. Decrease the heat to low, cover, and cook until the squash is tender, 15–20 minutes.

5. Stir in the parsley and cilantro and season with salt and pepper. Serve hot.

CHUNKY SUMMER ratatouille

4 tablespoons (60 ml) extra-virgin olive oil

5 cloves garlic, sliced

3 medium zucchini (courgettes), halved lengthwise, and cut into 1-inch (2.5-cm) pieces

1 large red bell pepper (capsicum), seeded and cut into 1/2-inch (1-cm) strips

1 red onion, thinly sliced

1 white onion, thinly sliced

1 tablespoon coriander seeds, coarsely crushed

1 pound (500 g) cherry tomatoes, halved

2 tablespoons thyme leaves

3 tablespoons finely chopped fresh parsley

Sea salt flakes

8 ounces (250 g) green beans, trimmed and halved

8 ounces (250 g) sugar snaps or snow peas (mangetout), trimmed

5 ounces (150 g) baby fava (broad) beans

Freshly squeezed juice of 1 lemon

Freshly ground black pepper

Serves 6 • Preparation 20 minutes • Cooking 40–45 minutes
Difficulty 1

1. Heat 2 tablespoons of oil in a large saucepan over medium heat. Add half the garlic and sauté for 1 minute. Add the zucchini and sauté until lightly browned, about 5 minutes. Lift out and place on paper towels to drain.

2. Sauté the bell pepper in the same oil until slightly browned, 3–5 minutes. Lift out and set aside with the zucchini.

3. Reduce the heat, pour in the remaining oil, and add both onions. Sauté over low heat until soft, 8–10 minutes. Add the remaining garlic and coriander, and sauté for 1 minute.

4. Add the tomatoes, thyme, and 2 tablespoons of parsley. Season with salt. Cover and cook until the tomatoes are soft, about 10 minutes. Add the green beans and simmer for 5 minutes. Add the sugar snaps and fava beans.

5. Return the zucchini and peppers to the pan. Bring the vegetables back to the simmering point. Simmer, uncovered, until all the vegetables are soft, 8–10 minutes. Season with salt, pepper, and lemon juice. Sprinkle with the remaining parsley. Serve warm or at room temperature.

The main ingredients in this dish—zucchini, leeks, and tomatoes—are all counted as non-starchy vegetables for the classic diabetes diet, which means you can eat them freely everyday.

ZUCCHINI & PESTO gratin

Pesto

2	cups (100 g) fresh basil leaves + extra leaves, to garnish the dish
2	tablespoons pine nuts
2	cloves garlic
1/2	cup (120 ml) extra-virgin olive oil
	Salt and freshly ground black pepper
4	tablespoons freshly grated Parmesan cheese

Gratin

1	pound (500 g) zucchini (courgettes), trimmed and sliced lengthwise about 1/8 inch (3 mm) thick
4	medium leeks, trimmed and thinly sliced
4	tomatoes, thinly sliced
4	tablespoons (60 ml) light (single) cream
2	cloves garlic, finely chopped
	Pinch of cayenne
	Freshly ground sea salt and black pepper
1	cup (150 g) fine dry bread crumbs
5	tablespoons finely grated Parmesan, Gruyère or other tasty, hard cheese
2	tablespoons extra-virgin olive oil, to drizzle

Serves 4-6 • Preparation 15 minutes • Cooking 20–30 minutes
Difficulty 1

Pesto

1. Combine the basil, pine nuts, garlic, oil, salt, and pepper in a food processor and chop until smooth. Transfer the mixture to a medium bowl and stir in the cheese.

Gratin

1. Preheat the oven to 400°F (200°C/gas 6). Grease an 11-inch (28-cm) gratin dish.

2. Put the pesto in a bowl and toss the zucchini slices in it until lightly coated. Layer with the zucchini slices and leeks in the prepared dish, followed by the tomatoes.

3. Use the pesto bowl (including any pesto leftovers) to mix the cream with the garlic, cayenne, salt, and pepper. Spoon over the vegetables.

4. Mix the bread crumbs with the cheese, and sprinkle over the top. Drizzle with the oil.

5. Bake for 20–30 minutes, until the topping is golden and the vegetables are tender.

6. Season generously with black pepper and serve hot.

desserts

ANGEL FOOD CAKE
with lavender & rose petals

1	cup (150 g) cake flour
1/4	cup (30 g) cornstarch (cornflour)
12	large egg whites
1	cup (200 g) Splenda sugar blend sweetener
1 1/2	teaspoons cream of tartar
1/4	teaspoon salt
1	teaspoon vanilla extract (essence)
	Petals from 2 red or yellow roses, coarsely chopped + extra whole leaves, to decorate
2	tablespoons dried lavender

Serves 12 • Preparation 15 minutes • Cooking 40–45 minutes
Difficulty 2

1. Preheat the oven to 325°F (160°C/gas 3). Set out a 10-inch (25-cm) tube pan with a removable bottom.

2. Sift the flour and cornstarch into a large bowl.

3. Beat the egg whites in a large bowl with an electric mixer at low speed until just broken up and beginning to froth. Add the cream of tarter and salt and beat at medium speed until soft and billowy.

4. Keep the mixer at medium speed, and gradually add the Splenda, beating until glossy and smooth but not quite stiff. Add the vanilla.

5. Fold in the flour and cornstarch, adding 2–3 tablespoons at a time. Carefully fold in the rose petals and lavender.

6. Spoon the batter into the prepared pan. Gently tap the pan on the work surface to release any air bubbles.

7. Bake for 40–45 minutes, until golden brown and springy to the touch.

8. Let cool on a wire rack. Decorate with the extra rose petals. Slice and serve.

It is a common myth that if you have diabetes you shouldn't eat fruit. Some fruits do contain more sugar than others, but they are also packed with fiber, vitamins, and other nutrients that are essential for good health. The important thing is to learn how much of each type of fruit you can eat without causing your blood sugar levels to spike. Most common fruits, including berries, cherries, peaches, apricots, apples, oranges, and pears all have a low glycemic load. Ask your health carer for a list of low GI fruit, or search for a list online.

FRESH FRUIT cups

1²/₃	cups (400 g) fat-free or low-fat Greek-style plain yogurt
3	tablespoons honey
2	teaspoons finely grated unwaxed lemon zest
1	tablespoon freshly squeezed lemon juice
1	(2-inch/5-cm) piece fresh ginger, unpeeled
1	mango, peeled, pitted, and cut into small cubes
1	cup (150 g) fresh strawberries, chopped
1	cup (150 g) fresh raspberries
¹/₄	cup chopped fresh mint + extra leaves, to garnish
6	amaretti cookies, coarsely crumbled

Serves 6 • Preparation 15 minutes • Difficulty 1

1. Combine the yogurt, 1 tablespoons of honey, and lemon zest in a bowl and set aside.

2. Finely grate the ginger into a small bowl. Squeeze through a fine-mesh sieve or strainer placed over a bowl to get a total of 1 tablespoon of ginger juice. Discard the pulp.

3. Add the remaining tablespoon of honey and the lemon juice to the bowl with the ginger and stir well. Add the mango, strawberries, and raspberries, tossing to coat.

4. Spoon half the fruit and juices among six large serving glasses. Spoon in the yogurt mixture and sprinkle with mint. Top with the remaining fruit and garnish with the extra mint leaves.

5. Sprinkle with the amaretti, and serve.

If you liked this recipe, you will love these as well.

BERRYFRUIT gazpacho

CHERRY & BLUEBERRY POTS with nut brittle

HONEY-ROASTED PEACHES with yogurt & sherry cream

BERRYFRUIT gazpacho

4 cups (600 g) mixed berries (strawberries, raspberries, cherries, blueberries, redcurrants), pitted, stalks removed, and halved as required + a few reserved, to garnish

2 tablespoons raw sugar

Finely grated zest of 1 unwaxed orange

Finely grated zest of 1 unwaxed lemon

4 teaspoons cornstarch (cornflour)

3 tablespoons cold water

½ cup (120 g) fat-free or low-fat Greek-style plain or vanilla yogurt, to serve (optional)

Serves 6 • Preparation 15 minutes + 12 hours to chill • Cooking 5–10 minutes • Difficulty 2

1. Put all the prepared berries into a bowl and mix with the sugar, orange zest, and lemon zest. Cover and chill overnight in the refrigerator. The fruit will release its juices during this time.

2. Strain the juices through a fine-mesh sieve, reserving the fruit. Put the juice in a saucepan over low heat and bring to a gentle boil.

3. Mix the cornstarch and water in a bowl until smooth. Add the boiling fruit juice to this mixture then return to the pan over medium heat, stirring constantly until the sauce has thickened, 2–3 minutes.

4. Add the fruit juice to the reserved fruit and divide among six serving bowls. Chill until ready to serve.

5. Serve cold, with a dollop of yogurt, if liked.

CHERRY & BLUEBERRY POTS with nut brittle

Nut Brittle

2	tablespoons sugar
1/2	cup (60 g) chopped almonds or pecans

Fruit

3	tablespoons sugar
1/3	cup (90 ml) cherry juice, from a carton
3	tablespoons red wine
	Finely grated zest and juice of 1 unwaxed orange
2	cups (300 g) fresh cherries, pitted
2	cups (300 g) blueberries
2	cups (500 ml) plain yogurt or crème fraîche
1	tablespoon acacia honey

Serves 6–8 • Preparation 15 minutes • Cooking 15 minutes • Difficulty 2

Nut Brittle

1. Melt the sugar in a small pan over low heat, stirring constantly. Add the nuts and stir until the sugar is golden. Spread out on a sheet of parchment paper and let cool.

2. Chop up when cold, and set aside.

Fruit

1. Stir the sugar in a heavy-bottomed pan over low heat until caramelized. Add the cherry juice, wine, and orange juice. Stir in the orange zest, cherries, and blueberries. Bring to a boil then simmer until the liquid has reduced and thickened, 3–4 minutes. Remove from the heat and set aside to cool.

2. Mix the yogurt with the honey. Arrange the dessert in layers in six to eight serving glasses. Put fruit in the bottom, cover with yogurt, followed by more fruit and yogurt. Sprinkle with the nut brittle, and serve.

Serve these peaches during the summer when fresh, locally grown fruit is at its best.

HONEY-ROASTED PEACHES
with yogurt & sherry cream

6   ripe yellow peaches, halved and pitted

1   cup (250 ml) freshly squeezed orange juice

     Freshly squeezed juice of 1 lemon

4   tablespoons (60 ml) dry sherry

4   tablespoons (60 ml) orange-blossom honey + extra, as required

6   amaretti cookies, crushed

     Handful of chopped almonds

1/2 cup (50 g) old fashioned rolled oats

1   tablespoon raw sugar

1   tablespoon confectioners' (icing) sugar

1/2 cup (120 g) fat-free or low-fat Greek-style plain yogurt

Serves 6 • Preparation 15 minutes • Cooking 15–20 minutes • Difficulty 1

1. Preheat the oven to 400°F (200°C/gas 6). Butter an ovenproof dish large enough to fit the peach halves in a snug single layer.

2. Combine the orange and lemon juices in a bowl. Add 2 tablespoons of sherry and stir in the honey to make a thick syrup. Put the peaches cut-side up in the dish.

3. Combine the amaretti, almonds, and oats in a bowl with the raw sugar. Press the mixture into the peaches.

4. Pour the orange syrup over the top, making sure each peach half is coated and remains upright. Bake for 15–20 minutes, until tender.

5. Whisk the confectioners' sugar and sherry into the yogurt.

6. Serve the peaches warm with the yogurt cream.

If you liked this recipe, you will love these as well.

GRILLED MANGO
with syrup

GRILLED PEARS
with dukkah

GRILLED MANGO with syrup

Serves 4 • Preparation 15 minutes • Cooking 5–10 minutes
Difficulty 1

	Freshly squeezed juice of 6 limes	1	(1/2-inch/1-cm) piece ginger, peeled and sliced
2	tablespoons brown sugar		
2	kaffir lime leaves, thinly sliced	2	firm ripe mangoes
		2	tablespoons melted butter, to brush

1. Combine the lime juice, jaggery, kaffir lime leaves, and ginger in a small saucepan over medium heat and bring to a boil. Simmer on low until syrupy, about 5 minutes. Strain through a fine-mesh sieve.

2. Preheat a grill pan (griddle) on medium-high heat.

3. Slice the mangos down either side of the pit to remove the cheeks. Score the flesh in a criss-cross pattern. Brush with the melted butter.

4. Grill, flat-side down first, until heated through and marked with lines, about 3 minutes each side.

5. Serve warm with the lime and ginger syrup.

COFFEE granita

Serves 6–8 • Preparation 15 minutes + 6–8 hours to freeze
Difficulty 2

1/4	cup (50 g) sugar	1/2	cup (120 ml) fat-free or low-fat Greek-style plain yogurt
11/2	cups (375 ml) very hot strong black coffee		

1. Place the sugar in a medium bowl. Pour the hot coffee over the top and stir until the sugar has completely dissolved. Pour the mixture into a medium bowl. Refrigerate until cooled, about 30 minutes.

2. Pour the mixture into a shallow freezerproof container. Cover with plastic wrap (cling film). Freeze until almost solid, 1–2 hours.

3. Use a fork or hand-held beater to break up into large crystals. Replace in the freezer until almost frozen again, about 1 hour, then break it up again with a fork. Repeat three or four times, until the crystals are separate and completely frozen.

4. Scoop into small glasses or cups, top with a dollop of yogurt, and serve.

GRILLED PEARS with dukkah

Serves 4 • Preparation 15 minutes • Cooking 5–10 minutes
Difficulty 1

1	teaspoon coriander seeds		seeds, lightly toasted
1	teaspoon cardamom seeds	3/4	cup (180 g) low-fat Greek-style plain yogurt
1/2	teaspoon whole black peppercorns	2	teaspoons rose water
1/2	cup (80 g) pistachios, finely chopped	4	ripe pears
2	tablespoons sesame	2	tablespoons melted butter, to brush
		2–3	tablespoons honey, warmed

1. Preheat a grill pan (griddle) on medium-high heat.

2. Dry-fry the coriander, cardamom, and peppercorns in a small frying pan over medium heat for 1 minute. Transfer to a mortar and pestle or spice grinder and blend to make a coarse powder. Combine the spices, pistachios, and sesame in a small bowl and set aside.

3. Combine the yogurt and rose water in a small bowl. Cover and refrigerate until required.

4. Cut the pears in half lengthwise and, using a teaspoon, scoop out the core. Brush with butter and grill until softened and marked with lines, 2–3 minutes on each side.

5. Serve the pears warm with a dollop of yogurt. Drizzle with the honey and sprinkle with the dukkah.

STRAWBERRIES with lemon

Serves 6 • Preparation 10 minutes + 1 hour to chill
Difficulty 1

4	cups (600 g) fresh strawberries	1/3	cup (90 ml) freshly squeezed lemon juice
2	tablespoons brown sugar		

1. If the strawberries are large, cut them into halves or quarters. Place in a serving dish.

2. Sprinkle with the sugar and drizzle with the lemon juice. Stir well.

3. Cover the bowl and chill in the refrigerator for at least 1 hour before serving.

Now you can enjoy this classic dessert without worrying about blood sugar levels. Each portion has about 100 calories, and 20 grams of carbohydrates.

CRÈME caramel

$1/2$	cup (100 g) sugar
1	tablespoon hot water
2	cups (500 ml) fat-free (skimmed) milk
$1/8$	teaspoon salt
$1/2$	cup cholesterol-free egg substitute
$1/2$	teaspoon vanilla extract (essence)
$1/4$	teaspoon maple extract

Serves 6 • Preparation 20 minutes + 4–12 hours to chill • Cooking 40–45 minutes • Difficulty 2

1. Heat $1/4$ cup (50 g) of sugar in a heavy-based saucepan over low heat, stirring constantly until melted and amber colored.

2. Remove from the heat and stir in the water. Return to the heat and stir until the mixture turns a dark caramel color. Divide evenly among six $1/2$-cup (120-ml) ramekins.

3. Preheat the oven to 350°F (180°C/gas 4).

4. Combine the milk, remaining $1/4$ cup of sugar with the salt in a medium bowl. Add the egg substitute and vanilla and maple extracts, mixing well.

5. Pour the mixture into the ramekins over the caramelized sugar. Place in a baking dish and pour in enough boiling water to come half way up the sides of the ramekins.

6. Bake for 40–45 minutes, until the custards are almost firm. Let cool completely on a wire rack.

7. Refrigerate 4 hours, or overnight. Just before serving, run a knife around edge of each ramekin. Invert the crème caramels onto serving dishes, and serve.

APPLE & BLACKBERRY crumble

Fruit

3	medium cooking apples, peeled, cored, and sliced
12	ounces (350 g) fresh blackberries
2	tablespoons light brown sugar
	Freshly squeezed juice of 1 lemon

Crumble Topping

1	cup (150 g) whole-wheat (wholemeal) flour
½	cup (50 g) rolled oats
⅓	cup 90 g) salted butter, chilled and diced
3	tablespoons raw sugar
½	teaspoon vanilla extract (essence)

Serves 6 • Preparation 20 minutes • Cooking 30–40 minutes • Difficulty 1

Fruit

1. Preheat the oven to 350°F (180°C/gas 4). Butter a 9-inch (23-cm) pie pan or ovenproof dish.

2. Put the fruit in the prepared pan. Sprinkle with the sugar and lemon juice and toss together.

Crumble Topping

1. Combine the flour and oats in a bowl. Rub in the butter with your fingertips until you have a lumpy, buttery mixture.

2. Stir in the sugar and vanilla extract with a fork. Sprinkle the topping over the fruit.

3. Bake for 30–40 minutes, until the topping is crisp and golden. Serve the crumble warm.

CLAFOUTIS

1 pound (500 g) black cherries, stems removed

4 tablespoons (60 ml) Kirsch or dark rum, for soaking

$^1/_2$ cup (75 g) all-purpose (plain) flour or amaranth flour (for a gluten-free dish)

$^1/_3$ cup (75 g) superfine (caster) sugar

2 free-range eggs

$1^1/_2$ cups (370 ml) low-fat (semi-skimmed) milk

4 tablespoons (60 g) unsalted butter, melted

1-2 tablespoons confectioners' (icing) sugar, for dusting

Serves 6 • Preparation 20 minutes + 1 hour to soak • Cooking 25–30 minutes • Difficulty 1

1. Put the cherries into a bowl and sprinkle with 2 tablespoons of the Kirsch. Let soak for 1 hour.

2. Combine the flour and sugar in a medium bowl. Beat in the egg yolks, milk, and 3 tablespoons of butter until smooth.

3. Drain the cherries, and add the Kirsch juice to the batter.

4. Whisk the egg whites in a clean bowl until stiff. Fold into the batter.

5. Preheat the oven to 375°F (190°C/gas 5). Brush the remaining butter on the bottom and sides of a 9-inch (23-cm) pie pan or an ovenproof dish. The dish should be large enough to hold the cherries in one layer.

6. Put the cherries in the pan and shake to distribute them evenly. Pour in the batter and shake again to level.

7. Bake for 25–30 minutes, until golden, puffed, and set in the center.

8. Remove from the oven and sprinkle with the remaining 2 tablespoons of Kirsch. Let cool for 15 minutes. Dust with the confectioners' sugar, and serve.

These healthy muffins are packed with fiber and goodness. Serve them warm anytime, from breakfast and bunch to dessert.

OAT BRAN muffins

2	cups (500 ml) unsweetened applesauce
1/2	cup (60 g) dates, pitted and chopped
1	cup (150 g) wheat bran
1/2	cup (120 ml) low-fat milk
1	large free-range egg
2	tablespoons honey
1	teaspoon finely grated fresh ginger
1/2	teaspoon vanilla extract (essence)
1/2	cup (75 g) all-purpose (plain) flour
2	tablespoons ground flaxseeds
1 1/4	teaspoons baking soda (bicarbonate of soda)
1/4	teaspoon sea salt flakes
1/4	teaspoon ground allspice
1/4	cup (30 g) rolled oats

Makes 24 • Preparation 15 minutes • Cooking 30–40 minutes
Difficulty 2

1. Preheat the oven to 375°F (190°C/gas 5). Lightly grease two 12-cup mini-muffin pans.

2. Combine the applesauce and dates in a medium saucepan over medium heat, stirring frequently, until the mixture is reduced to about 1 1/4 cups, 15–20 minutes.

3. Spread in an even layer on a rimmed baking sheet, and let cool completely.

4. Transfer to a large bowl, and stir in the bran, milk, egg, honey, ginger, and vanilla. Let stand for 10 minutes.

5. Combine the flour, flaxseeds, baking soda, salt, allspice, and oats in a bowl. Stir into the bran mixture. Spoon the batter into the prepared pans, filling to the brims.

6. Bake for 15–20 minutes, until a toothpick inserted into the centers comes out clean. Let cool in the pans for 10 minutes. Serve warm.

If you liked this recipe, you will love these as well.

HONEY-ROASTED PEACHES with yogurt & sherry cream

CLAFOUTIS

CHOCOLATE ZUCCHINI muffins

The zucchini in these muffins adds fiber and texture to the crumb of these tasty muffins. It also adds moisture, which means they are equally good when served the day after baking.

CHOCOLATE ZUCCHINI muffins

1/2	cup (120 g) unsalted butter, melted and cooled
1	cup (200 g) granulated Splenda sweetener
1	large free-range egg
1/2	teaspoon vanilla extract (essence)
1	cup (100 g) finely grated zucchini
3	tablespoons low-fat sour cream
1	cup (150 g) all-purpose (plain) flour
1/4	cup (30 g) unsweetened cocoa powder
1/2	teaspoon sea salt flakes
3 1/2	ounces (100 g) dark chocolate, grated
12	walnut halves

Serves 12 • Preparation 15 minutes • Cooking 20–25 minutes
Difficulty 1

1. Preheat the oven to 350°F (180°C/gas 4). Lightly grease a standard 12-cup muffin pan.

2. Beat the butter, Splenda, and egg in a bowl until well combined. Stir in the vanilla, zucchini, and sour cream. Sift the flour, cocoa, and salt into a bowl, then stir into the batter. Stir in the chocolate.

3. Spoon the batter into the prepared pan, filling each muffin cup about two-thirds full. Press a walnut half into the top of each muffin.

4. Bake for 20–25 minutes, until a toothpick inserted into the centers comes out clean.

5. Let the muffins cool slightly in the pan on a wire rack, then turn out onto the rack and let cool completely.

If you liked this recipe, you will love these as well.

ANGEL FOOD CAKE
with lavender & rose petals

APPLE & BLACKBERRY
crumble

OAT BRAN
muffins

INDEX